STECK-VAUGHN

TABE®
Fundamentals

Focus on Skills

Math Computation

LEVEL D

2nd Edition

Steck Vaughn™

HOUGHTON MIFFLIN HARCOURT
Supplemental Publishers

www.SteckVaughn.com
800-531-5015

Photo Credits: Page iv: ©Bluestone Productions/SuperStock Royalty Free; 2: ©Photodisc/Getty Images Royalty Free; 4: ©Veer Royalty Free.

Reviewers

Victor Gathers
Regional Coordinator of Adult Services
New York City Department of Education
Brooklyn Adult Learning Center
Brooklyn, New York

Brannon Lentz
Assistant Director of Adult Education/Skills Training
Northwest Shoals Community College
Muscle Shoals, Alabama

Jean Pierre-Pipkin, Ed.D.
Director of Beaumont I.S.D. Adult Education
Cooperative Consortium
Beaumont, Texas

Special thanks to Wayne Couvillion for sharing his enthusiasm and love of math with us.

ISBN-13: 978-1-4190-5359-7
ISBN-10:   1-4190-5359-0

7 8 9   1689   15 14 13 12
4500354431

Contents

To the Learner

Congratulations on your decision to study for the TABE! You are taking an important step in your educational career. This book will help you do your best on the TABE. You'll also find hints and strategies that will help you prepare for test day. Practice these skills—your success lies in your hands.

What Is the TABE?

TABE stands for the Tests of Adult Basic Education. These paper-and-pencil tests, published by McGraw-Hill, measure your progress on basic skills. There are five tests in all: Reading, Mathematics Computation, Applied Mathematics, Language, and Spelling.

TABE Levels M, D, and A

Test	Number of Items	Suggested Working Time (in minutes)
1 Reading	50	50
2 Mathematics Computation	25	15
3 Applied Mathematics	50	50
4 Language	55	39
5 Spelling	20	10

Test 1 Reading

This test measures basic reading skills. The main concepts covered by this test are word meaning, critical thinking, and understanding basic information.

Many things on this test will look familiar to you. They include documents and forms necessary to your everyday life, such as directions, bank statements, maps, and consumer labels. The test also includes items that measure your ability to find and use information from a dictionary, table of contents, or library computer display. The TABE also tests a learner's understanding of fiction and nonfiction passages.

Test 2 Mathematics Computation

Test 2 covers adding, subtracting, multiplying, and dividing. On the test you must use these skills with whole numbers, fractions, decimals, integers, and percents.

The skills covered in the Mathematics Computation test are the same skills you use daily to balance your checkbook, double a recipe, or fix your car.

Test 3 Applied Mathematics

The Applied Mathematics test links mathematical ideas to real-world situations. Many things you do every day require basic math. Making budgets, cooking, and doing your taxes all take math. The test also covers pre-algebra, algebra, and geometry. Adults need to use all of these skills.

Some questions will relate to one theme. For example, auto repairs could be the subject and the question could focus on the repair schedule. You may be told when a car was last repaired and how often it needs to be repaired. You might be asked to predict the next maintenance date.

Many of the items will not require you to use a specific strategy or formula to get the correct answer. Instead this test challenges you to use your own problem-solving strategies to answer the question.

Test 4 Language

The Language test asks you to analyze different types of writing. Examples are business letters, resumes, job reports, and essays. For each task, you have to show you understand good writing skills.

The questions fit adult interests and concerns. Some questions ask you to think about what is wrong in the written material. In other cases, you will correct sentences and paragraphs.

Test 5 Spelling

In everyday life, you need to spell correctly, especially in the workplace. The spelling words on this test are words that many people misspell and words that are commonly used in adult writing.

Test-Taking Tips

1. Read the directions very carefully. Make sure you read through them word for word. If you are not sure what the question says, ask the person giving the test to explain it to you.

2. Read each question carefully. Make sure you know what it means and what you have to do.

3. Read all of the answers carefully, even if you think you know the answer.

4. Make sure that the reading supports your answer. Don't answer without checking the reading. Don't rely only on outside knowledge.

5. Answer all of the questions. If you can't find the right answer, rule out the answers that you know are wrong. Then try to figure out the right answer. If you still don't know, make your best guess.

6. If you can't figure out the answer, put a light mark by the question and come back to it later. Erase your marks before you finish.

7. Don't change an answer unless you are sure your first answer is wrong. Usually your first idea is the correct answer.

8. If you get nervous, stop for a while. Take a few breaths and relax. Then start working again.

How to Use *TABE Fundamentals*

Step-by-Step Instruction In Levels M and D, each lesson starts with step-by-step instruction on a skill. The instruction contains examples and then a test example with feedback. This instruction is followed by practice questions. Work all of the questions in the lesson's practice and then check your work in the Answers and Explanations in the back of the book.

The Level A books contain practice for each skill covered on the TABE. Work all of the practice questions and then check your work in the Answers and Explanations in the back of the book.

Reviews The lessons in Levels M and D are grouped by a TABE Objective. At the end of each TABE Objective, there is a Review. Use these Reviews to find out if you need to review any of the lessons before continuing.

Performance Assessment At the end of every book, there is a special section called the Performance Assessment. This section is similar to the TABE test. It has the same number and type of questions. This assessment will give you an idea of what the real test is like.

Answer Sheet At the back of the book is a practice bubble-in answer sheet. Practice bubbling in your answers. Fill in the answer sheet carefully. For each answer, mark only one numbered space on the answer sheet. Mark the space beside the number that corresponds to the question. Mark only one answer per question. On the real TABE, if you have more than one answer per question, they will be scored as incorrect. Be sure to erase any stray marks.

Strategies and Hints Pay careful attention to the TABE Strategies and Hints throughout this book. Strategies are test-taking tips that help you do better on the test. Hints give you extra information about a skill.

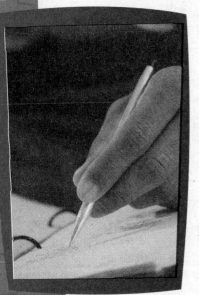

Setting Goals

On the following page is a form to help you set your goals. Setting goals will help you get more from your work in this book.

Section 1. Why do you want to do well on the TABE? Take some time now to set your short-term and long-term goals on page 3.

Section 2. Making a schedule is one way to set priorities. Deadlines will help you stay focused on the steps you need to take to reach your goals.

Section 3. Your goals may change over time. This is natural. After a month, for example, check the progress you've made. Do you need to add new goals or make any changes to the ones you have? Checking your progress on a regular basis helps you reach your goals.

> For more information on setting goals, see Steck-Vaughn's *Start Smart Goal Setting Strategies*.

Math Computation

1. Set Your Goals

What is your long-term goal for using this book?

_____
_____
_____
_____

Complete these areas to identify the smaller steps to take to reach your long-term goal.

Content area	What I Know	What I Want to Learn
Reading	_____	_____
Language	_____	_____
Spelling	_____	_____
Math	_____	_____
Other	_____	_____

2. Make a Schedule

Set some deadlines for yourself.

> For a 20-week planning calendar, see Steck-Vaughn's *Start Smart Planner*.

Goals	Begin Date	End Date
_____	_____	_____
_____	_____	_____
_____	_____	_____
_____	_____	_____

3. Celebrate Your Success

Note the progress you've made. If you made changes in your goals, record them here.

_____
_____
_____
_____

To the Instructor

About TABE

The Tests of Adult Basic Education are designed to meet the needs of adult learners in ABE programs. Written and designed to be relevant to adult learners' lives and interests, this material focuses on the life, job, academic, and problem-solving skills that the typical adult needs.

Because of the increasing importance of thinking skills in any curriculum, *TABE Fundamentals* focuses on critical thinking throughout each TABE Objective.

The TABE identifies the following thinking processes as essential to learning and achieving goals in daily life:

- ✦ Gather Information
- ✦ Organize Information
- ✦ Analyze Information
- ✦ Generate Ideas
- ✦ Synthesize Elements
- ✦ Evaluate Outcomes

Test 1 Reading

The TABE measures an adult's ability to understand home, workplace, and academic texts. The ability to construct meaning from prose and visual information is also covered through reading and analyzing diagrams, maps, charts, forms, and consumer materials.

Test 2 Mathematics Computation

This test covers whole numbers, decimals, fractions, integers, percents, and algebraic expressions. Skills are carefully targeted to the appropriate level of difficulty.

Test 3 Applied Mathematics

This test emphasizes problem-solving and critical-thinking skills, with a focus on the life-skill applications of mathematics. Estimation and pattern-recognition skills also are important on this test.

Test 4 Language

The Language test focuses on writing and effective communication. Students examine writing samples that need revision, with complete-sentence and paragraph contexts for the various items. The test emphasizes editing, proofreading, and other key skills. The context of the questions are real-life settings appropriate to adults.

Test 5 Spelling

This test focuses on the words learners most typically misspell. In this way, the test identifies the spelling skills learners most need in order to communicate effectively. Items typically present high-frequency words in short sentences.

Uses of the TABE

There are three basic uses of the TABE:

Instructional

From an instructional point of view, the TABE allows instructors to assess students' entry levels as they begin an adult program. The TABE also allows instructors to diagnose learners' strengths and weaknesses in order to determine appropriate areas to focus instruction. Finally the TABE allows instructors and institutions to monitor learners' progress.

Administrative

The TABE allows institutions to assess classes in general and measure the effectiveness of instruction and whether learners are making progress.

Governmental

The TABE provides a means of assessing a school's or program's effectiveness.

The National Reporting System (NRS) and the TABE

Adult education and literacy programs are federally funded and thus accountable to the federal government. The National Reporting System monitors adult education. Developed with the help of adult educators, the NRS sets the reporting requirements for adult education programs around the country. The information collected by the NRS is used to assess the effectiveness of adult education programs and make necessary improvements.

A key measure defined by the NRS is educational gain, which is an assessment of the improvement in learners' reading, writing, speaking, listening, and other skills during their instruction. Programs assess educational gain at every stage of instruction.

NRS Functioning Levels	Grade Levels	TABE (7–8) scaled scores
Beginning ABE Literacy	0–1.9	Reading . . . . 367 and below Total Math . . . . 313 and below Language . . . . . 392 and below
Beginning Basic Education	2–3.9	Reading . . . . 368–460 Total Math . . . . 314–441 Language 393–490
Low Intermediate Basic Education	4–5.9	Reading . . . . 461–517 Total Math . . . 442–505 Language 491–523
High Intermediate Basic Education	6–8.9	Reading . . . . 518–566 Total Math . . . . 506–565 Language 524–559
Low Adult Secondary Education	9–10.9	Reading . . . . 567–595 Total Math . . . 566–594 Language 560–585

According to the NRS guidelines, states select the method of assessment appropriate for their needs. States can assess educational gain either through standardized tests or through performance-based assessment. Among the standardized tests typically used under NRS guidelines is the TABE, which meets the NRS standards both for administrative procedures and for scoring.

The three main methods used by the NRS to collect data are the following:

1. **Direct program reporting,** from the moment of student enrollment
2. **Local follow-up surveys,** involving learners' employment or academic goals
3. **Data matching,** or sharing data among agencies serving the same clients so that outcomes unique to each program can be identified.

Two of the major goals of the NRS are academic achievement and workplace readiness. Educational gain is a means to reaching these goals. As learners progress through the adult education curriculum, the progress they make should help them either obtain or keep employment or obtain a diploma, whether at the secondary school level or higher. The TABE is flexible enough to meet both the academic and workplace goals set forth by the NRS.

Using *TABE Fundamentals*

Adult Basic Education Placement

From the outset, the TABE allows effective placement of learners. You can use the *TABE Fundamentals* series to support instruction of those skills where help is needed.

High School Equivalency

Placement often involves predicting learners' success on the GED, the high school equivalency exam. Each level of *TABE Fundamentals* covers Reading, Applied and Computational Math, Language, and Spelling, to allow learners to focus their attention where it is needed.

Assessing Progress

Each TABE skill is covered in a lesson. These lessons are grouped by TABE Objective. At the end of each TABE Objective, there is a Review. Use these Reviews to find out if the learners need to review any of the skills before continuing.

At the end of the book, there is a special section called the Performance Assessment. This section is similar to the TABE test. It has the same number and type of questions. You can use the Performance Assessment as a timed pretest or posttest with your learners, or as a more general review for the actual TABE.

Steck-Vaughn's *TABE Fundamentals* Program at a Glance

The charts on the following page provide a quick overview of the elements of Steck-Vaughn's *TABE Fundamentals* series. Use this chart to match the TABE objectives with the skill areas for each level. This chart will come in handy whenever you need to find which objectives fit the specific skill areas you need to cover.

Steck-Vaughn's *TABE Fundamentals* Program at a Glance

	Level M		Level D		Level A
	Reading	Language and Spelling	Reading	Language and Spelling	Reading, Language, and Spelling
Reading					
Interpret Graphic Information	♦		♦		♦
Words in Context	♦		♦		♦
Recall Information	♦		♦		♦
Construct Meaning	♦		♦		♦
Evaluate/Extend Meaning	♦		♦		♦
Language					
Usage		♦		♦	♦
Sentence Formation		♦		♦	♦
Paragraph Development		♦		♦	♦
Punctuation and Capitalization		♦		♦	♦
Writing Convention		♦		♦	♦
Spelling					
Vowel		♦		♦	♦
Consonant		♦		♦	♦
Structural Unit		♦		♦	♦

	Level M		Level D		Level A
	Math Computation	Applied Math	Math Computation	Applied Math	Computational and Applied Math
Mathematics Computation					
Addition of Whole Numbers	♦				
Subtraction of Whole Numbers	♦				
Multiplication of Whole Numbers	♦		♦		
Division of Whole Numbers	♦		♦		
Decimals	♦		♦		♦
Fractions	♦		♦		♦
Integers			♦		♦
Percents			♦		♦
Orders of Operation					♦
Applied Mathematics					
Number and Number Operations		♦		♦	♦
Computation in Context		♦		♦	♦
Estimation		♦		♦	♦
Measurement		♦		♦	♦
Geometry and Spatial Sense		♦		♦	♦
Data Analysis		♦		♦	♦
Statistics and Probability		♦		♦	♦
Patterns, Functions, Algebra		♦		♦	♦
Problem Solving and Reasoning		♦		♦	♦

Lesson 1 | Multiplication of Whole Numbers—Regrouping

On the TABE you will be asked to multiply two numbers, which may be arranged horizontally rather than vertically. To make multiplying easier, place the greater number above the smaller one, making sure the numbers are lined up by place value.

$$\begin{array}{r} 135 \\ \times\ \ 6 \end{array}$$ ← In 135, 5 is in the ones place, 3 is in the tens place, and 1 is in the hundreds place.

Example Multiply. 547 × 15 =

Step 1. Line up the numbers by place value. Multiply each digit of the top number by the digit in the ones place in the bottom number (547 × 5).

$$\begin{array}{cccc} & \text{hundreds} & \text{tens} & \text{ones} \\ & 2 & 3 & \\ & 5 & 4 & 7 \\ \times & & 1 & 5 \\ \hline 2 & 7 & 3 & 5 \end{array}$$

Step 2. Multiply each digit of the top number by the 1 of the bottom number. Because the 1 is in the tens place, put a 0 in the ones place.

$$\begin{array}{ccccc} \text{thousands} & \text{hundreds} & \text{tens} & \text{ones} \\ & 5 & 4 & 7 \\ \times & & 1 & 5 \\ \hline 2 & 7 & 3 & 5 \\ 5 & 4 & 7 & 0 \end{array}$$

Step 3. Add to find the answer.

$$\begin{array}{ccccc} \text{thousands} & \text{hundreds} & \text{tens} & \text{ones} \\ & 5 & 4 & 7 \\ \times & & 1 & 5 \\ \hline & 1 & 1 & \\ 2 & 7 & 3 & 5 \\ + 5 & 4 & 7 & 0 \\ \hline 8 & 2 & 0 & 5 \end{array}$$

547 × 15 = 8,205

Test Example

Multiply. Circle the answer.

1

    75 × 37 =

    A 2,675

    B 2,775

    C 2,745

    D 2,645

    E None of these

1 B

$$\begin{array}{r} 1 \\ 3 \\ 75 \\ \times\ 37 \\ \hline 525 \\ +\ 2250 \\ \hline 2775 \end{array}$$

Hint

When you multiply, each digit of the top number must be multiplied by each digit of the bottom number.

Multiply. Circle the answer.

1

43
× 5

A 205
B 215
C 315
D 220
E None of these

2

327 × 3 =

F 981
G 1,161
H 961
J 1,181
K None of these

3

631
× 73

A 45,963
B 44,063
C 47,263
D 46,063
E None of these

4

5,331 × 24 =

F 129,744
G 127,944
H 128,744
J 124,944
K None of these

5

75
× 4

A 300
B 280
C 400
D 305
E None of these

6

63 × 54 =

F 3,302
G 3,392
H 3,202
J 3,392
K None of these

7

508
× 4

A 2,302
B 2,072
C 2,002
D 2,032
E None of these

8

649 × 500 =

F 300,500
G 32,450
H   3,245
J 324,500
K None of these

9

74 × 52 =

A 3,648
B 3,898
C 3,848
D 3,488
E None of these

10

762
× 8

F 6,906
G 6,096
H 5,686
J 5,696
K None of these

Check your answers on page 59.

Lesson 2 Division of Whole Numbers—No Remainder

If you want to divide 756 bushels of apples evenly among 6 delivery trucks, you can use division to figure out how many bushels to place in each truck. Division problems are written in two ways: with a division sign 756 ÷ 6 =, or with a division bracket 6)756.

Example Divide. 756 ÷ 6 =

Step 1. Set up the problem using the division bracket. You must decide how many 6s there are in 7. There is only one 6, so write the 1 above the 7 in the hundreds column. Then multiply 1 × 6 = 6. Write the 6 below the 7 and subtract 7 – 6 = 1. Then bring down the 5.

```
    hundreds tens ones
        1
    6 )7    5    6
      – 6   ↓
        1   5
```

Step 2. Multiply 2 × 6 = 12. Write the 2 above the 5 in the tens column. Write the 12 below the 15 and subtract. Then bring the 6 down.

```
    hundreds tens ones
        1    2
    6 )7    5    6
      – 6
        1    5
       –1    2    ↓
             3    6
```

Step 3. Multiply 6 × 6 = 36. Write the 6 above the 6 in the division bracket. Write 36 below the 36 and subtract. 36 – 36 = 0. There are no more numbers to bring down.

```
    hundreds tens ones
        1    2    6
    6 )7    5    6
      – 6
        1    5
       –1    2    ↓
             3    6
            –3    6
             0
```

756 ÷ 6 = 126. Each delivery truck will carry 126 bushels of apples.

Test Example

Divide. Circle the answer.

1

7)5,376

A 753
B 770
C 710
D 768
E None of these

```
1   D      768
         4 13
        7)5376
         – 49
           47
         – 42
           56
         – 56
            0
```

TABE Strategy

Use multiplication to check your answers. Multiply the number you divided by with your answer. For example, check 5,376 ÷ 7 = 768: 768 × 7 = 5,376.

Divide. Circle the answer.

1

$232 \div 4 =$

A 58
B 48
C 59
D 57
E None of these

6

$17\overline{)510}$

F 3
G 40
H 4
J 35
K None of these

2

$5\overline{)85}$

F 10
G 18
H 17
J 15
K None of these

7

$372 \div 4 =$

A 93
B 83
C 84
D 90
E None of these

3

$57 \div 19 =$

A 5
B 4
C 3
D 7
E None of these

8

$378 \div 6 =$

F 62
G 91
H 63
J 61
K None of these

4

$6,552 \div 4 =$

F 1,638
G 1,613
H 1,110
J 1,788
K None of these

9

$3\overline{)75}$

A 25
B 21
C 33
D 35
E None of these

5

$130 \div 5 =$

A 20
B 34
C 25
D 26
E None of these

10

$695 \div 5 =$

F 111
G 149
H 139
J 131
K None of these

Check your answers on page 59.

Lesson 3 | Division of Whole Numbers—Remainder

When one number doesn't divide evenly into another, you have an amount left over. The number left over is called a remainder. Use the letter "R" to show a remainder. $7 \div 3 = 2$ R1 says that when you divide 7 by 3, the answer is 2 with a remainder of 1.

Example   Divide. 30 ÷ 4 =

Step 1. Set up the problem using a division bracket. Because 4 is larger than 3, divide 30 by 4. How many 4s are there in 30? There are 7. Write 7 above the 0. Multiply $7 \times 4 = 28$. Write 28 under 30, and subtract. $30 - 28 = 2$.

```
    tens ones
           7
4 ) 3   0
  - 2   8
        2
```

Step 2. Look at the number 2. Because 4 is larger than 2, you can't divide, and there are no more numbers to bring down. The 2 is the amount left over, or the remainder.

```
    tens ones
           7
4 ) 3   0
  - 2   8
        2
```

$30 \div 4 = 7$ R2

Test Example

Divide. Circle the answer.

1

$7 \overline{)53}$

- A   7
- B   6 R1
- C   10 R3
- D   7 R4
- E   None of these

```
1  D      7 R4
        7)53
        - 49
           4
```

Solve. Circle the answer.

1

$65 \div 9 =$

A 6 R2
B 7 R1
C 7 R2
D 8
E None of these

2

$87 \div 6 =$

F 14 R2
G 19
H 15 R3
J 11 R1
K None of these

3

$246 \div 7 =$

A 40 R6
B 36
C 35 R1
D 30 R6
E None of these

4

$14\overline{)589}$

F 42 R1
G 40 R2
H 42
J 40 R9
K None of these

5

$12\overline{)347}$

A 27 R1
B 28
C 28 R1
D 28 R11
E None of these

6

$6\overline{)59}$

F 19 R5
G 8 R3
H 9 R5
J 10
K None of these

7

$60 \div 7 =$

A 8 R4
B 9 R4
C 9
D 7
E None of these

8

$188 \div 7 =$

F 24
G 26 R6
H 26 R7
J 27 R6
K None of these

9

$78 \div 5 =$

A 17
B 15 R3
C 14
D 11 R3
E None of these

10

$8\overline{)413}$

F 51 R5
G 51 R8
H 52
J 52 R5
K None of these

Check your answers on pages 59–60.

Solve. Circle the answer.

1 $324 \div 3 =$

A 109
B 101
C 106
D 107
E None of these

2 $17 \times 94 =$

F 1,698
G 1,578
H 1,598
J 1,597
K None of these

3 $5\overline{)37}$

A 5 R2
B 7 R2
C 6 R1
D 7 R3
E None of these

4 $556 \times 2 =$

F 1,202
G 1,012
H 1,112
J 1,002
K None of these

5
$$\begin{array}{r} 742 \\ \times\ \ 15 \\ \hline \end{array}$$

A 10,130
B 11,130
C 10,930
D 11,120
E None of these

6 $13\overline{)104}$

F 80
G 13
H 9
J 8
K None of these

7 $95 \times 65 =$

A 5,875
B 6,155
C 5,175
D 6,175
E None of these

8 $7,752 \div 3 =$

F 2,580
G 2,584
H 2,210
J 2,517
K None of these

9 $2\overline{)65}$

A 321
B 30 R3
C 310 R2
D 312
E None of these

10

$98 \div 4 =$

    F   24 R2
    G   42 R2
    H 440 R4
    J 242
    K None of these

11

$42 \times 9,167 =$

    A 385,014
    B 374,914
    C 383,914
    D 382,704
    E None of these

12

$392 \div 7 =$

    F 54
    G 50
    H 65
    J 55
    K None of these

13

$85 \div 17 =$

    A   3
    B 15
    C 10
    D   5
    E None of these

14

$\begin{array}{r} 909 \\ \times \quad 6 \\ \hline \end{array}$

    F 6,363
    G 5,404
    H 5,454
    J 5,514
    K None of these

15

$75 \div 4 =$

    A 11 R1
    B 17
    C 10 R5
    D 18 R3
    E None of these

16

$931 \times 307 =$

    F 295,127
    G 285,817
    H   34,447
    J   43,757
    K None of these

17

$71 \div 8 =$

    A 8 R7
    B 6
    C 7 R8
    D 80
    E None of these

18

$6\overline{)78}$

    F 13
    G 15
    H 19
    J 11
    K None of these

Check your answers on pages 60–61.

Lesson 4 ▷ Addition of Decimals

Did you know that you use decimal numbers every day? If you had $1.75 and found $0.25, you would add decimals to find out how much money you had. The period in $1.75 is called a decimal point. By learning a few simple rules to use with decimals, you will be ready to solve decimal problems on the TABE.

Example Use rules of addition to add decimals. 2.33 + 0.74 =

Step 1. Place one number under the other, lining up the decimal points. Write a decimal point in the answer line so that it lines up with the other decimal points.

$$\begin{array}{r} 2.33 \\ +.74 \\ \hline \end{array}$$

Step 2. Add the numbers just like you were adding whole numbers (numbers without decimals). Regroup just like you do with regular addition.

$$\begin{array}{r} 2.33 \\ +0.74 \\ \hline .7 \end{array}$$

Step 3. Add the numbers in the next column to the left. Regroup if necessary.

$$\begin{array}{r} {}^{1} \\ 2.33 \\ +0.74 \\ \hline .07 \end{array}$$

Step 4. Add the next column. Don't forget to add the 1 you regrouped.

$$\begin{array}{r} {}^{1} \\ 2.33 \\ +0.74 \\ \hline 3.07 \end{array}$$

2.33 + 0.74 = 3.07

Test Example

Add. Circle the answer.

1
$$\begin{array}{r} 4.6 \\ +2.08 \\ \hline \end{array}$$

A 6.86
B 7.4
C 6.68
D 6.4
E None of these

1 C $$\begin{array}{r} 4.60 \\ +2.08 \\ \hline 6.68 \end{array}$$

Hint

Make sure that the decimal numbers have the same number of digits to the right of the decimal point before you begin adding. Place 0s at the end of the shorter number until each number has the same amount of digits to the right of the decimal point.

Add. Circle the answer.

1

$$\begin{array}{r} 7.342 \\ +\ 2.526 \end{array}$$

A 9.3568
B 9.868
C 9.224
D 9.086
E None of these

6

$$\begin{array}{r} 3.75 \\ +\ 0.66 \end{array}$$

F 4.31
G 4.41
H 5.31
J 4.36
K None of these

2

$$\begin{array}{r} 7.46 \\ +\ 0.23 \end{array}$$

F 7.96
G 9.36
H 9.76
J 7.7
K None of these

7

$$\begin{array}{r} 6.749 \\ +\ 4.610 \end{array}$$

A 10.1359
B 11.459
C 10.359
D 11.359
E None of these

3

$$\begin{array}{r} 4.35 \\ +\ 0.78 \end{array}$$

A 4.03
B 5.13
C 5.03
D 12.15
E None of these

8

$$\begin{array}{r} 9.03 \\ +\ 4.20 \end{array}$$

F 13.05
G 13.5
H 13.23
J 13.32
K None of these

4

$$\begin{array}{r} 7.03 \\ +\ 4.10 \end{array}$$

F 11.13
G 11.04
H 11.4
J 10.13
K None of these

9

$$\begin{array}{r} 4.1 \\ +\ 1.8 \end{array}$$

A 5.09
B 0.59
C 5.7
D 5.9
E None of these

5

$$\begin{array}{r} 237.943 \\ +\ 46.085 \end{array}$$

A 284.138
B 284.938
C 283.038
D 283.938
E None of these

10

$$\begin{array}{r} 0.84 \\ +\ 2.39 \end{array}$$

F 3.93
G 2.23
H 10.39
J 2.49
K None of these

Check your answers on page 61.

Lesson 5 | Subtraction of Decimals

When you left home you had $8.23 in your pocket. You just bought some juice for $1.09. To find out how much money you have left, you would subtract decimal numbers. Decimal subtraction is just like subtraction with whole numbers, except there is a decimal point.

Example Use the rules of subtraction to subtract decimal numbers.
$8.23 − $1.09 =

Step 1. Write the numbers in columns, putting the smaller number under the larger one so that the decimal points are lined up. Write a decimal point in the answer line under the other decimal points.

$$8.23$$
$$-1.09$$

Step 2. Subtract, starting from the right. Borrow and regroup from the next column to the left, just like regular subtraction. $13 − 9 = 4$.

$$\overset{1\ 13}{8.2\rlap{/}3}$$
$$-1.09$$
$$.\ 4$$

Step 3. Subtract the next column to the left. Because you took one away from the 2, you now have a 1 instead of a 2, so $1 − 0 = 1$. Write the 1 below the line under the 0.

$$\overset{1\ 13}{8.\rlap{/}2\rlap{/}3}$$
$$-1.09$$
$$.14$$

Step 4. Subtract the next column. $8 − 1 = 7$.

$$\overset{1\ 13}{8.\rlap{/}2\rlap{/}3}$$
$$-1.09$$
$$7.14$$

$8.23 − $1.09 = $7.14. You have **$7.14** left in your pocket.

Test Example

Subtract. Circle the answer.

1

$28 − 0.062 =$

A 27.038

B 27.938

C 28.062

D 27.38

E None of these

Hint

You can add a decimal point and zeros after a whole number without changing the value of the number. $28 = 28.000$

$$
\begin{array}{r}
\overset{7\ 9\ 9\ 10}{28.0\rlap{/}0\rlap{/}0} \\
-\ \ 0.062 \\
\hline
27.938
\end{array}
$$

1 B

Subtract. Circle the answer.

1

$$\begin{array}{r} 36 \\ -0.024 \end{array}$$

A 36.024
B 35.975
C 35.976
D 35.876
E None of these

6

$$\begin{array}{r} 9.02 \\ -0.54 \end{array}$$

F 3.62
G 9.52
H 8.48
J 9.56
K None of these

2

$$\begin{array}{r} 7.04 \\ -0.39 \end{array}$$

F 6.65
G 7.35
H 6.61
J 4.14
K None of these

7

$$\begin{array}{r} 6.008 \\ -0.292 \end{array}$$

A 5.706
B 6.296
C 6.716
D 5.716
E None of these

3

$$\begin{array}{r} 6 \\ -1.68 \end{array}$$

A 7.68
B 5.68
C 4.32
D 4.31
E None of these

8

$$\begin{array}{r} 3.51 \\ -3.27 \end{array}$$

F 0.46
G 0.34
H 0.23
J 0.24
K None of these

4

$$\begin{array}{r} 6.93 \\ -6.48 \end{array}$$

F 0.45
G 0.15
H 0.55
J 0.44
K None of these

9

$$\begin{array}{r} 52 \\ -0.058 \end{array}$$

A 52.022
B 51.922
C 50.412
D 51.642
E None of these

5

$$\begin{array}{r} 8.43 \\ -6.25 \end{array}$$

A 2.38
B 2.22
C 2.28
D 2.17
E None of these

10

$$\begin{array}{r} 4.532 \\ -2.151 \end{array}$$

F 2.481
G 2.381
H 2.371
J 2.421
K None of these

Check your answers on page 61.

Lesson 6 Multiplication of Decimals

Multiplication of decimals is just like multiplication of whole numbers, except that you must be careful to put the decimal point in the correct place in the answers.

Example Multiply. 0.6 × 3.2 =

Step 1. Multiply 32 × 6.

$$
\begin{array}{r}
^1\ ^1 \\
3.2 \\
\times\quad 0.6 \\
\hline
1\,9\,2
\end{array}
$$

Step 2. Next multiply by the 0. Then add to find the answer.

$$
\begin{array}{r}
^1\ ^1 \\
3.2 \\
\times\quad 0.6 \\
\hline
1\,9\,2 \\
+\quad 0\,0\,0 \\
\hline
1\,9\,2
\end{array}
$$

Step 3. Now you will find out where to put the decimal point in the answer. Count the number of decimal places in the numbers you multiplied.

3.2 ⟶ **1 place**

× 0.6 ⟶ **+ 1 place**

2 places

Step 4. There must be the same amount of decimal places in the answer as there is in the numbers you multiplied. If there aren't enough decimal places in the answer, write zeros to the left of the answer. In this case, there is no need to add any zeros.

$$
\begin{array}{r}
^1\ ^1 \\
3.2 \longrightarrow \text{1 place}\\
\times\quad 0.6 \longrightarrow \text{1 place}\\
\hline
1\,9\,2 \\
+\quad 0\,0\,0 \\
\hline
1.9\,2 \longrightarrow \text{2 places}
\end{array}
$$

0.6 × 3.2 = 1.92

Test Example

Multiply. Circle the answer.

1   2.4
  × 1.5

    A 1.0

    B 3.6

    C 3.9

    D 1.1

    E None of these

1 B
$$
\begin{array}{r}
^{1\ 2} \\
2.4 \\
\times\quad 1.5 \\
\hline
1\,20 \\
+\quad 2\,40 \\
\hline
3.60
\end{array}
$$

Multiply. Circle the answer.

1

$$\begin{array}{r} 7 \\ \times\ 0.3 \\ \hline \end{array}$$

- A 4.242
- B 2.21
- C 11
- D 2.1
- E None of these

2

$$\begin{array}{r} 0.8 \\ \times\ 3.0 \\ \hline \end{array}$$

- F 3.8
- G 0.24
- H 3.24
- J 2.4
- K None of these

3

$$\begin{array}{r} 7.2 \\ \times\ 1.3 \\ \hline \end{array}$$

- A 8.5
- B 3.16
- C 2.16
- D 9.36
- E None of these

4

$$\begin{array}{r} 3.1 \\ \times\ 4.2 \\ \hline \end{array}$$

- F 7.3
- G 13.02
- H 12.02
- J 13.62
- K None of these

5

$$\begin{array}{r} 0.7 \\ \times\ 0.5 \\ \hline \end{array}$$

- A 35
- B 0.12
- C 1.2
- D 0.035
- E None of these

6

$$\begin{array}{r} 5.2 \\ \times\ 8.0 \\ \hline \end{array}$$

- F 40.6
- G 13.2
- H 41.6
- J 13.62
- K None of these

7

$$\begin{array}{r} 6.8 \\ \times\ 4.1 \\ \hline \end{array}$$

- A 27.88
- B 24.88
- C 10.9
- D 27.2
- E None of these

8

$$\begin{array}{r} 8 \\ \times\ 0.3 \\ \hline \end{array}$$

- F 24
- G 2.4
- H .24
- J 0.024
- K None of these

9

$$\begin{array}{r} 5.3 \\ \times\ 2.1 \\ \hline \end{array}$$

- A 10.13
- B 7.4
- C 11.13
- D 11.103
- E None of these

10

$$\begin{array}{r} 6.3 \\ \times\ 1.2 \\ \hline \end{array}$$

- F 7.65
- G 5.1
- H 16.30
- J 1.86
- K None of these

Check your answers on page 61.

Division of Decimals

You multiply and divide decimals to find out your gas mileage, total cost in dollars and cents, or the monthly payments on your charge cards. Dividing decimals is similar to division with whole numbers, but you must remember to put the decimal point in the right place. On the TABE you will be asked to divide decimal numbers.

Example Divide. 728 ÷ 0.14 =

Step 1. Move the decimal point in the number 0.14 to the right two places. 0.14 becomes 14. Now move the decimal point in 728 two places to the right. 728 becomes 72800.

$$0.14.\overline{)728.00.}$$

Step 2. Now that the decimals are moved, divide like you do with whole numbers. Divide 14 into 72. How many 14s are there in 72? There are 5. Place the 5 above the 2. Multiply 5 × 14 = 70. Write 70 below the 72 and subtract. 72 − 70 = 2. Then bring down the 8.

$$\begin{array}{r} 5 \\ 14\overline{)72800.} \\ -70 \\ \hline 28 \end{array}$$

Step 3. 14 divides into 28 two times. Write 2 above the 8. Multiply 2 × 14 = 28. Write 28 below the 28, and subtract. 28 − 28 = 0.

$$\begin{array}{r} 52 \\ 14\overline{)72800.} \\ -70 \\ \hline 28 \\ -28 \\ \hline 0 \end{array}$$

Step 4. Because 14 goes into 0 zero times and there are only 0s left to divide, you can bring down the other zeros. Write a zero above each 0 in the bracket. Put the decimal point in the answer directly above the decimal point in the bracket.

$$\begin{array}{r} 5200. \\ 14\overline{)72800.} \\ -70 \\ \hline 28 \\ -28 \\ \hline 00 \\ -00 \\ \hline 00 \end{array}$$

728 ÷ 0.14 = 5200

Test Example

Divide. Circle the answer.

1

$$0.43\overline{)559}$$

A	130
B	1,300
C	1.3
D	13
E	None of these

1 B

$$\begin{array}{r} 1300.0 \\ 043\overline{)55900.0} \\ -43 \\ \hline 129 \\ -129 \\ \hline 0 \end{array}$$

Divide. Circle the answer.

1

8)0.04

A 0.5
B 5.5
C 55
D 0.55
E None of these

6

0.04)732

F 0.0183
G 1.83
H 0.00183
J 1.183
K None of these

2

0.21)252

F 0.12
G 0.012
H 12
J 1,200
K None of these

7

0.39)819

A 210
B 2,100
C 2.1
D 21
E None of these

3

16)3.18

A 1.9875
B 19.875
C 0.19875
D 0.19857
E None of these

8

60)1.68

F 0.082
G 0.289
H 0.028
J 2.80
K None of these

4

25)3.02

F 1.208
G 0.1208
H 12.808
J 0.0128
K None of these

9

15)3.63

A 0.242
B 24.2
C 242
D 0.0242
E None of these

5

0.26)780

A 3,000
B 3.303
C 0.033
D 30
E None of these

10

0.74)111

F 1,500
G 1.05
H 15
J 0.015
K None of these

Check your answers on pages 61–62.

Solve. Circle the correct answer.

1

$$\begin{array}{r} 3.7 \\ +\ 2.2 \\ \hline \end{array}$$

A 5.9
B 0.59
C 5.72
D 5.27
E None of these

2

$0.09\overline{)756}$

F 84
G 8.4
H 8,400
J 0.084
K None of these

3

$$\begin{array}{r} 57 \\ -\ 0.039 \\ \hline \end{array}$$

A 57.039
B 56.061
C 56.61
D 56.961
E None of these

4

$$\begin{array}{r} 6.05 \\ +\ 0.93 \\ \hline \end{array}$$

F 6.98
G 15.35
H 6.99
J 7.43
K None of these

5

$$\begin{array}{r} 6.5 \\ \times\ 3.3 \\ \hline \end{array}$$

A 214.5
B 21.45
C 20.45
D 3.2
E None of these

6

$20\overline{)1.57}$

F 78.5
G 7.625
H 8.75
J 0.0857
K None of these

7

$$\begin{array}{r} 5.74 \\ -\ 5.36 \\ \hline \end{array}$$

A 0.42
B 0.38
C 0.37
D 0.48
E None of these

8

$$\begin{array}{r} 9.751 \\ +\ 0.592 \\ \hline \end{array}$$

F .243
G 10.433
H 9.343
J 11.953
K None of these

9

$72\overline{)9.36}$

   A 13
   B 0.013
   C 1.3
   D 0.13
   E None of these

14

$\begin{array}{r} 4.2 \\ \times\ \ 8 \\ \hline \end{array}$

   F 33.6
   G 3.36
   H 0.326
   J 3.136
   K None of these

10

$\begin{array}{r} 7.6 \\ \times\ \ 4 \\ \hline \end{array}$

   F 0.304
   G 30.4
   H 0.0304
   J 3.04
   K None of these

15

$\begin{array}{r} 8.701 \\ +\ 3.041 \\ \hline \end{array}$

   A 12.12
   B 11.472
   C 10.472
   D 11.742
   E None of these

11

$\begin{array}{r} 5.000 \\ -\ 0.450 \\ \hline \end{array}$

   A 5.450
   B 4.550
   C 5.540
   D 4.440
   E None of these

16

$\begin{array}{r} 7.1 \\ \times\ 8.2 \\ \hline \end{array}$

   F 58.22
   G 15.3
   H 56.8
   J 14.2
   K None of these

12

$0.64\overline{)248}$

   F 38.75
   G 3.875
   H 387.5
   J 0.3875
   K None of these

17

$9\overline{)9.54}$

   A 0.16
   B 1.106
   C 0.0106
   D 1.06
   E None of these

13

$\begin{array}{r} 8.9 \\ +\ 4.3 \\ \hline \end{array}$

   A 12.2
   B 12.12
   C 13.2
   D 13.3
   E None of these

18

$\begin{array}{r} 8.04 \\ -\ 0.28 \\ \hline \end{array}$

   F 7.75
   G 7.67
   H 5.24
   J 8.24
   K None of these

Check your answers on pages 62–63.

Lesson 8 ▸ Addition of Fractions

Adding fractions can be very helpful if you are trying to name the parts of a whole. You may add fractions when using a ruler, buying cloth, or figuring out the number of hours you worked in a week. Here are the parts of a fraction.

$$\frac{3}{4} \begin{array}{l} \leftarrow \text{numerator} \\ \leftarrow \text{fraction bar} \\ \leftarrow \text{denominator} \end{array}$$

On the TABE you'll see fraction problems in vertical and horizontal form.

vertical form	**horizontal form**
$\begin{array}{r} \frac{6}{10} \\ +\frac{2}{10} \\ \hline \end{array}$	$\frac{6}{10} + \frac{2}{10} =$

Example Add. $\dfrac{9}{16} + \dfrac{7}{16} =$

Step 1. Write out the problem, placing the numbers side by side. Add a fraction bar after the = sign.

$$\frac{9}{16} + \frac{7}{16} = \text{—}$$

Step 2. Look at the denominators. Because both denominators are the same, the answer will have the same denominator. Write 16 under the fraction bar.

$$\frac{9}{16} + \frac{7}{16} = \frac{}{\mathbf{16}}$$

Step 3. Add the numerators. $9 + 7 = 16$. Write 16 above the fraction bar. When the top number and the bottom number are the same, you have 1 whole.

$$\frac{9}{16} + \frac{7}{16} = \frac{\mathbf{16}}{16} = \mathbf{1}$$

$$\frac{9}{16} + \frac{7}{16} = \mathbf{1}$$

Example Add. $3\dfrac{2}{3} + 5\dfrac{3}{4} =$

Step 1. Write out the problem in the vertical form. It is easier to add the whole numbers together and the fractions together.

$$\begin{array}{r} 3\frac{2}{3} \\ +\ 5\frac{3}{4} \\ \hline \end{array}$$

Step 2. When the two fractions have different denominators, change the fractions to **equivalent fractions**. That means they must have the same denominator before you can begin adding. Fractions that equal the same amount are called equivalent fractions. For example $\frac{1}{2} = \frac{2}{4}$.

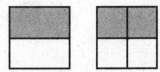

You can find an equivalent fraction by multiplying or dividing both the numerator and the denominator by the same number. First compare the denominators. Both 3 and 4 divide evenly into 12: $3 \times 4 = 12$ and $4 \times 3 = 12$.

$$3\frac{2}{3} \times 4 = \overline{12}$$

$$+ 5\frac{3}{4} \times 3 = \overline{12}$$

Step 3. To find the new numerators, multiply by the same numbers. Then add.

$$3\frac{2 \times 4}{3} = \frac{8}{12}$$

$$+ 5\frac{3 \times 3}{4} = \frac{9}{12}$$

$$8 \qquad \frac{17}{12} = 8\frac{17}{12}$$

Step 4. Simplify $\frac{17}{12}$. To do this, divide 17 by 12: $17 \div 12 = 1$ R 5. Since $\frac{17}{12} = 1\frac{5}{12}$, add 1 to the whole numbers.

$$\overset{1}{3}\frac{2}{3}$$

$$+ 5\frac{3}{4}$$

$$9\frac{5}{12}$$

Test Example

Add. Circle the answer.

1   $\frac{7}{12} + \frac{3}{12} =$

    A $\frac{3}{4}$

    B $\frac{5}{12}$

    C $\frac{5}{6}$

    D $\frac{9}{12}$

    E None of these

Hint

Make sure the fraction is in the lowest terms already before choosing "None of these."

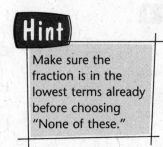

1 C

$$\frac{7}{12} + \frac{3}{12} = \frac{10}{12} = \frac{5}{6}$$

Add. Circle the answer.

1

$$\frac{3}{14}$$
$$+\frac{8}{14}$$

A $\frac{11}{14}$

B $\frac{11}{28}$

C $1\frac{1}{14}$

D $\frac{17}{22}$

E   None of these

2

$$\frac{3}{4}$$
$$+\frac{2}{8}$$

F $\frac{4}{8}$

G $\frac{5}{12}$

H $\frac{2}{4}$

J 1

K   None of these

3

$$\frac{11}{18}$$
$$+\frac{7}{18}$$

A $1\frac{1}{18}$

B 1

C $1\frac{4}{25}$

D $\frac{1}{2}$

E   None of these

4

$$\frac{8}{27}$$
$$+\frac{10}{27}$$

F $\frac{2}{9}$

G $\frac{35}{37}$

H $\frac{2}{3}$

J $\frac{19}{27}$

K   None of these

5

$$\frac{2}{3}$$
$$+\frac{5}{6}$$

A $\frac{9}{12}$

B $\frac{7}{9}$

C $\frac{1}{2}$

D $\frac{1}{6}$

E   None of these

6

$$6\frac{4}{5}$$
$$+5\frac{2}{4}$$

F $12\frac{3}{10}$

G $11\frac{3}{10}$

H $11\frac{1}{3}$

J $1\frac{1}{2}$

K   None of these

7

$$\frac{9}{19}$$
$$+\frac{5}{19}$$

A $1\frac{1}{6}$

B $\frac{15}{19}$

C $\frac{7}{9}$

D $\frac{14}{19}$

E   None of these

8

$$2\frac{95}{100}$$
$$+3\frac{3}{10}$$

F $5\frac{98}{100}$

G $6\frac{1}{4}$

H $5\frac{1}{4}$

J $6\frac{1}{5}$

K   None of these

Check your answers on page 63.

Lesson 9 Subtraction of Fractions

If you and your friends started with 2 cakes and ate $\frac{4}{8}$ of one cake, how much cake would you have left? Subtracting fractions will help you solve this problem. You can subtract $\frac{4}{8}$ from 2 to figure out what fraction of the cake is left.

Example Subtract. $2 - \frac{4}{8} =$

Step 1. Every whole number is a fraction with a denominator of 1, so $2 = \frac{2}{1}$. Write the whole number 2 as an equivalent fraction with the same denominator as the given fraction: 8. To do this, multiply both the numerator and denominator of the whole number by the factor that will give the denominator 8.

$$\frac{2}{1} \times \frac{8}{8} = \frac{16}{8}$$

Step 2. Look at the denominators. Because both numbers are the same, the answer will have the same denominator. Write 8 under the fraction bar.

$$\frac{16}{8} - \frac{4}{8} = \frac{}{8}$$

Step 3. Subtract the top numbers. $16 - 4 = 12$. Write 12 above the fraction bar. Reduce the fraction by finding a number that can be divided into the numerator and the denominator. Because there are three 4s in 12 and two 4s in 8, reduce the fraction by dividing the numerator and denominator by 4.

$$\frac{16}{8} - \frac{4}{8} = \frac{12}{8} \div \frac{4}{4} = \frac{3}{2}$$

Step 4. Simplify $\frac{3}{2}$. To do this, divide 3 by 2: $3 \div 2 = 1$ R 1. This means $\frac{3}{2} = 1\frac{1}{2}$.

$$2 - \frac{4}{8} = 1\frac{1}{2}$$

Example Subtract. $6\frac{3}{4} - 3\frac{1}{4} =$

Step 1. Write out the problem in the vertical form.

$$\begin{array}{r} 6\frac{3}{4} \\ -\ 3\frac{1}{4} \\ \hline \end{array}$$

Step 2. The denominator of both numbers is 4, so the denominator of the answer will be 4, too. Now subtract the numerators $3 - 1 = 2$. Then subtract the whole numbers $6 - 3 = 3$.

$$\begin{array}{r} 6\frac{3}{4} \\ -\ 3\frac{1}{4} \\ \hline 3\frac{2}{4} \end{array}$$

Step 3. Reduce the fraction in the answer. Divide both the numerator and denominator by 2.

$$3\frac{2}{4} \div \frac{2}{2} = \frac{1}{2} = 3\frac{1}{2}$$

$$6\frac{3}{4} - 3\frac{1}{4} = 3\frac{1}{2}$$

Test Example

Subtract. Circle the answer.

1

$$\begin{array}{r} \frac{7}{9} \\ -\frac{4}{9} \\ \hline \end{array}$$

A 4

B $\frac{1}{6}$

C $\frac{2}{5}$

D $\frac{1}{3}$

E None of these

1 D $\begin{array}{r} \frac{7}{9} \\ -\frac{4}{9} \\ \hline \frac{3}{9} \end{array}$

$$\frac{3}{9} \div \frac{3}{3} = \frac{1}{3}$$

TABE Strategy

If you finish the test early, **check** your answers by reworking every problem.

Subtract. Circle the answer.

1

$$\begin{array}{r} 1 \phantom{\frac{5}{9}} \\ - \frac{5}{9} \\ \hline \end{array}$$

A $\frac{1}{3}$

B $\frac{1}{9}$

C $\frac{2}{3}$

D $\frac{4}{9}$

E None of these

2

$$\begin{array}{r} 7 \frac{4}{5} \\ - 1 \frac{2}{10} \\ \hline \end{array}$$

F $6 \frac{4}{5}$

G $5 \frac{3}{5}$

H $6 \frac{2}{5}$

J $6 \frac{3}{5}$

K None of these

3

$$\begin{array}{r} \frac{4}{5} \\ - \frac{2}{5} \\ \hline \end{array}$$

A $\frac{3}{5}$

B $\frac{1}{3}$

C $\frac{3}{10}$

D $\frac{1}{5}$

E None of these

4

$$\begin{array}{r} 8 \frac{3}{4} \\ - 6 \frac{1}{2} \\ \hline \end{array}$$

F $2 \frac{3}{4}$

G $2 \frac{1}{4}$

H $3 \frac{1}{4}$

J $2 \frac{1}{2}$

K None of these

5

$$\begin{array}{r} \frac{4}{9} \\ - 1 \frac{1}{3} \\ \hline \end{array}$$

A $\frac{4}{9}$

B $\frac{1}{9}$

C $\frac{1}{3}$

D $\frac{2}{9}$

E None of these

6

$$\begin{array}{r} 3 \phantom{\frac{2}{6}} \\ - 2 \frac{2}{6} \\ \hline \end{array}$$

F $\frac{5}{6}$

G $\frac{2}{3}$

H $5 \frac{1}{3}$

J 1

K None of these

7

$$\begin{array}{r} 7 \phantom{\frac{2}{7}} \\ - 1 \frac{2}{7} \\ \hline \end{array}$$

A $\frac{3}{7}$

B $\frac{6}{7}$

C $5 \frac{5}{7}$

D $5 \frac{2}{7}$

E None of these

8

$$\begin{array}{r} 4 \frac{5}{8} \\ - 2 \frac{3}{8} \\ \hline \end{array}$$

F $2 \frac{3}{8}$

G $2 \frac{1}{2}$

H $2 \frac{1}{4}$

J $2 \frac{1}{8}$

K None of these

Check your answers on page 63.

Multiplication of Fractions

On the TABE you will be asked to multiply fractions and whole numbers. Multiplying fractions is different than adding or subtracting fractions because you have to multiply both the numerator and the denominator. Both fractions don't need to have the same denominator when you multiply them.

Example Multiply. $\frac{3}{5} \times \frac{7}{1} =$

Step 1. Multiply the numerators. $3 \times 7 = 21$. Write 21 above the fraction bar.

$$\frac{3}{5} \times \frac{7}{1} = \textbf{21}$$

Step 2. Now multiply the denominators. $5 \times 1 = 5$. Write 5 below the fraction bar.

$$\frac{3}{5} \times \frac{7}{1} = \frac{21}{\textbf{5}}$$

Step 3. Simplify the answer. Because the numerator is larger than the denominator, you can divide the numerator by the denominator to simplify: $21 \div 5 = 4$ R1. The 4 is a whole number. The remainder of 1 becomes the numerator of the new fraction.

The denominator stays the same: $\frac{1}{5}$.

$$\frac{3}{5} \times \frac{7}{1} = \frac{21}{5} = 4\frac{1}{5}$$

Test Example

Multiply. Circle the answer.

1 $\frac{3}{4} \times \frac{1}{3} =$

    A $\frac{1}{12}$

    B $1\frac{1}{4}$

    C $\frac{1}{4}$

    D $1\frac{4}{9}$

    E None of these

1 C

$$\frac{3}{4} \times \frac{1}{3} = \frac{3}{12} = \frac{1}{4}$$

Multiply. Circle the answer.

1

$\frac{2}{5} \times \frac{2}{3} =$

A $\frac{4}{15}$

B $\frac{4}{10}$

C $\frac{2}{5}$

D $\frac{3}{10}$

E None of these

2

$\frac{5}{9} \times \frac{3}{4} =$

F $4\frac{5}{9}$

G $\frac{5}{72}$

H $4\frac{8}{9}$

J $4\frac{1}{3}$

K None of these

3

$\frac{5}{6} \times \frac{1}{2} =$

A $\frac{5}{6}$

B $\frac{7}{12}$

C $\frac{5}{12}$

D $3\frac{1}{3}$

E None of these

4

$\frac{2}{3} \times \frac{5}{1} =$

F $3\frac{1}{3}$

G $\frac{2}{15}$

H $1\frac{1}{3}$

J $3\frac{2}{3}$

K None of these

5

$\frac{3}{8} \times \frac{5}{8} =$

A $\frac{2}{8}$

B $\frac{15}{64}$

C $\frac{24}{40}$

D 1

E None of these

6

$\frac{3}{4} \times \frac{2}{9} =$

F $4\frac{1}{2}$

G $4\frac{3}{4}$

H $\frac{1}{12}$

J $3\frac{1}{4}$

K None of these

7

$\frac{1}{2} \times \frac{1}{6} =$

A $\frac{1}{18}$

B $3\frac{1}{2}$

C $\frac{1}{12}$

D $1\frac{1}{2}$

E None of these

8

$\frac{4}{5} \times \frac{2}{1} =$

F $5\frac{1}{5}$

G $\frac{1}{8}$

H $1\frac{3}{5}$

J $2\frac{3}{5}$

K None of these

Check your answers on page 63.

Lesson 11 | Division of Fractions

Have you ever needed to divide $1\frac{2}{4}$ casseroles equally among 9 people? You will find that knowing how to multiply fractions will help you divide fractions. For the TABE, you will need to know how to divide fractions by whole numbers and by other fractions.

Example Divide. $1\frac{2}{4} \div 9 =$

Step 1. Rewrite the whole number 9 as a fraction by putting it over 1: $\frac{9}{1}$. Then write the mixed number as an improper fraction. Multiply the denominator by the whole number and add the numerator. Write out the problem, placing the numbers side by side.

$$1\frac{2}{4} \div 9 = \frac{6}{4} \div \frac{9}{1}$$

Step 2. Flip the second fraction, so that the numerator is on the bottom and the denominator is on the top. Next change the division sign to a multiplication sign.

$$\frac{6}{4} \div \frac{9}{1} = \frac{6}{4} \times \frac{1}{9}$$

Step 3. Multiply the numerators, $6 \times 1 = 6$. Then multiply the denominators, $4 \times 9 = 36$.

$$\frac{6}{4} \div \frac{9}{1} = \frac{6}{4} \times \frac{1}{9} = \frac{6}{36}$$

Step 4. Reduce the fraction by dividing the top and bottom by the same number. Because there are two 3s in 6 and twelve 3s in 36, reduce the fraction by dividing both the numerator and denominator by 3.

$$\frac{6}{36} \div \frac{3}{3} = \frac{2}{12} = \frac{1}{6}$$

$$1\frac{2}{4} \div 9 = \frac{1}{6}$$

Test Example

Divide. Circle the answer.

1

$$\frac{4}{5} \div \frac{6}{1} =$$

A $4\frac{4}{5}$

B $\frac{2}{15}$

C $5\frac{1}{5}$

D $\frac{1}{6}$

E None of these

1 B

$$\frac{4}{5} \div \frac{6}{1} = \frac{4}{5} \times \frac{1}{6} = \frac{4}{30} = \frac{2}{15}$$

Divide. Circle the answer.

1

$2\frac{5}{6} \div 4 =$

A $3\frac{1}{3}$

B $\frac{1}{5}$

C $\frac{17}{24}$

D $2\frac{1}{3}$

E None of these

2

$\frac{3}{4} \div \frac{1}{2} =$

F $\frac{3}{8}$

G $\frac{1}{2}$

H $1\frac{1}{2}$

J $\frac{2}{3}$

K None of these

3

$3\frac{2}{3} \div 3 =$

A $\frac{1}{3}$

B 33

C $2\frac{1}{3}$

D $1\frac{2}{9}$

E None of these

4

$4\frac{2}{7} \div 5 =$

F $\frac{6}{7}$

G $\frac{8}{30}$

H $1\frac{3}{7}$

J $3\frac{3}{7}$

K None of these

5

$\frac{2}{3} \div \frac{5}{6} =$

A $\frac{5}{9}$

B $1\frac{1}{5}$

C $\frac{1}{5}$

D $1\frac{1}{4}$

E None of these

6

$\frac{4}{9} \div 5 =$

F $\frac{4}{45}$

G $2\frac{2}{9}$

H $2\frac{1}{3}$

J $\frac{1}{9}$

K None of these

7

$\frac{2}{7} \div \frac{3}{4} =$

A $\frac{3}{14}$

B $4\frac{2}{3}$

C $\frac{8}{21}$

D $2\frac{5}{8}$

E None of these

8

$\frac{1}{5} \div \frac{2}{3} =$

F $3\frac{1}{3}$

G $\frac{2}{15}$

H $7\frac{1}{2}$

J $\frac{3}{10}$

K None of these

Check your answers on page 63.

Solve. Circle the answer.

1

$$8 \frac{4}{9}$$
$$- 7 \frac{2}{9}$$

A $1\frac{1}{9}$

B $1\frac{4}{9}$

C $1\frac{2}{9}$

D $1\frac{1}{3}$

E None of these

2

$$\frac{3}{11}$$
$$+ \frac{7}{11}$$

F 1

G $\frac{7}{9}$

H $\frac{9}{11}$

J $\frac{5}{6}$

K None of these

3

$$\frac{2}{9} \div \frac{1}{3} =$$

A $\frac{2}{3}$

B $\frac{2}{27}$

C $1\frac{1}{2}$

D $\frac{2}{9}$

E None of these

4

$$\frac{5}{6} \times \frac{2}{3} =$$

F $2\frac{5}{6}$

G $\frac{5}{18}$

H $3\frac{1}{2}$

J $\frac{5}{9}$

K None of these

5

$$\frac{6}{8}$$
$$- \frac{1}{4}$$

A $\frac{1}{4}$

B $\frac{1}{3}$

C $\frac{1}{2}$

D $\frac{3}{8}$

E None of these

6

$$\frac{3}{4} \div \frac{5}{6} =$$

F $1\frac{1}{9}$

G $\frac{1}{10}$

H $\frac{5}{8}$

J $1\frac{3}{8}$

K None of these

7

$$\frac{2}{7} \times \frac{1}{4} =$$

A $\frac{3}{28}$

B $\frac{1}{7}$

C $\frac{2}{17}$

D $\frac{1}{14}$

E None of these

8

$$3 \frac{55}{100}$$
$$+ 4 \frac{8}{10}$$

F $8\frac{1}{4}$

G $7\frac{85}{100}$

H $8\frac{7}{20}$

J $7\frac{63}{100}$

K None of these

9

$$\begin{array}{r} 4 \\ -2\,\dfrac{1}{6} \\ \hline \end{array}$$

A $\dfrac{1}{6}$

B $1\,\dfrac{2}{3}$

C $\dfrac{5}{6}$

D $1\,\dfrac{5}{6}$

E None of these

10

$$\begin{array}{r} \dfrac{9}{22} \\ +\,\dfrac{13}{22} \\ \hline \end{array}$$

F $1\,\dfrac{1}{22}$

G $\dfrac{31}{35}$

H 1

J $\dfrac{1}{2}$

K None of these

11

$$3\,\dfrac{3}{5} \div 2 =$$

A $\dfrac{2}{5}$

B $1\,\dfrac{4}{5}$

C 1

D $1\,\dfrac{1}{5}$

E None of these

12

$$\begin{array}{r} 4\,\dfrac{1}{4} \\ +\,5\,\dfrac{2}{5} \\ \hline \end{array}$$

F $9\,\dfrac{13}{20}$

G $4\,\dfrac{5}{20}$

H $1\,\dfrac{9}{10}$

J $\dfrac{3}{10}$

K None of these

13

$$\begin{array}{r} 9 \\ -\,8\,\dfrac{1}{6} \\ \hline \end{array}$$

A $1\,\dfrac{1}{3}$

B $1\,\dfrac{5}{6}$

C $1\,\dfrac{3}{4}$

D $1\,\dfrac{1}{2}$

E None of these

14

$$\begin{array}{r} 2\,\dfrac{7}{25} \\ +\,1\,\dfrac{3}{5} \\ \hline \end{array}$$

F $1\,\dfrac{7}{25}$

G $3\,\dfrac{4}{5}$

H $3\,\dfrac{22}{25}$

J $3\,\dfrac{7}{8}$

K None of these

15

$$3\,\dfrac{7}{8} \div \dfrac{1}{6} =$$

A $5\,\dfrac{1}{4}$

B $23\,\dfrac{1}{4}$

C $5\,\dfrac{3}{8}$

D $\dfrac{1}{6}$

E None of these

16

$$\begin{array}{r} \dfrac{4}{7} \\ -\,\dfrac{3}{7} \\ \hline \end{array}$$

F $\dfrac{3}{4}$

G $\dfrac{2}{7}$

H $\dfrac{1}{7}$

J $\dfrac{1}{14}$

K None of these

Check your answers on pages 63–64.

Lesson 12 Addition of Integers

An integer may be a positive number such as 9 or a negative number such as ⁻7. Positive numbers can be written with or without a positive sign (+). For example, ⁺9 = 9. A negative number, however, must always include a negative sign (−) in front of the number. Here are some rules for adding integers.

- When two numbers have the same sign, add those numbers together and give the answer the same sign.
- When the signs of the numbers are different, subtract the lesser number from the greater. The answer has the sign of the greater number.

Example Add. ⁻6 + 10 =

Step 1. Add ⁻6 and 10 using the rules for adding numbers with different signs. Because the signs are different, subtract the smaller number from the larger number.

$$\begin{array}{r} 10 \\ -\ 6 \\ \hline 4 \end{array}$$

⁻6 + 10 = 4

Test Example

Add. Circle the answer.

1
    7 + ⁻5 =

      A   2
      B   ⁻2
      C ⁻12
      D   12
      E   None of these

TABE Strategy

Check your answer by drawing a number line and counting the spaces moved in the positive or negative direction.

1 A

7 + ⁻5 = 7 − 5 = 2

Add. Circle the answer.

1

$8 + {}^-3 =$

  A $^-5$
  B   11
  C   5
  D $^-11$
  E   None of these

6

$10 + {}^-7 =$

  F   17
  G $^-17$
  H $^-3$
  J   3
  K   None of these

2

$^-4 + 9 =$

  F   7
  G   13
  H $^-1$
  J   5
  K   None of these

7

$^-8 + 8 =$

  A   16
  B $^-8$
  C   6
  D $^-16$
  E   None of these

3

$9 + {}^-2 =$

  A   11
  B $^-7$
  C $^-11$
  D   7
  E   None of these

8

$3 + {}^-9 =$

  F   6
  G $^-6$
  H $^-11$
  J   11
  K   None of these

4

$4 + {}^-6 =$

  F $^-10$
  G   2
  H $^-2$
  J   10
  K   None of these

9

$^-7 + 5 =$

  A $^-12$
  B   12
  C $^-11$
  D $^-4$
  E   None of these

5

$^-9 + 13 =$

  A   10
  B   4
  C   22
  D $^-8$
  E   None of these

10

$^-8 + 7 =$

  F $^-1$
  G   15
  H $^-5$
  J $^-11$
  K   None of these

Check your answers on page 64.

Lesson 13 Subtraction of Integers

The opposite of going up 3 steps is going down 3 steps. In both cases the same distance is traveled: 3 steps. Integers include all whole numbers (positive numbers), their opposites (corresponding negative numbers), and 0. Integers that are the same except for sign are opposites. For example, ⁻3 is the opposite of ⁺3. The **absolute value** of an integer is its distance from 0. Absolute value is shown like this |⁻3|. On the TABE, absolute value expressions include subtraction of integers. Subtracting an integer is the same as adding its opposite.

Example   Subtract. 22 − ⁻4 =

Step 1. Choose the rule that matches the signs.

Signs with Subtraction	Rule	Examples
1. To subtract a positive number from a negative number ⁻9 − 6 =	Add the absolute values.	$\lvert^-9\rvert + \lvert^+6\rvert$ ↓ 9 + 6 = 15
	The difference is negative.	⁻9 − 6 = ⁻15
2. To subtract a negative number from a positive number 12 − ⁻4 =	Add the absolute values.	$\lvert 12\rvert + \lvert^-4\rvert$ ↓ 12 + 4 = 16
	The difference is positive.	12 − ⁻4 = 16

Step 2. Add the absolute values.

$\lvert^+22\rvert = 22$

$\lvert^-4\rvert = 4$

22 + 4 = 26

Step 3. The difference is positive.

22 − ⁻4 = **26**

22 − ⁻4 = 26

Test Example

Subtract. Circle the answer.

1
   5 − ⁻6 =

   A ⁻11
   B ⁻1
   C 11

   D 1
   E None of these

Hint

The absolute value of a number is always positive.

1 C

5 − ⁻6 = 5 + ⁺6 = 11

Subtract. Circle the answer.

1

$27 - {}^{-}5 =$

A 32
B ${}^{-}32$
C 22
D ${}^{-}22$
E None of these

6

${}^{-}8 - 13 =$

F 5
G ${}^{-}5$
H ${}^{-}20$
J 20
K None of these

2

$7 - {}^{-}8 =$

F ${}^{-}15$
G 15
H ${}^{-}1$
J 1
K None of these

7

$3 - {}^{-}10 =$

A ${}^{-}7$
B ${}^{-}13$
C 13
D 7
E None of these

3

${}^{-}9 - 16 =$

A ${}^{-}7$
B 7
C ${}^{-}25$
D 25
E None of these

8

$18 - {}^{-}4 =$

F 24
G ${}^{-}24$
H ${}^{-}14$
J 14
K None of these

4

$8 - {}^{-}5 =$

F 13
G ${}^{-}3$
H ${}^{-}13$
J 3
K None of these

9

$3 - {}^{-}7 =$

A 10
B ${}^{-}10$
C ${}^{-}4$
D 4
E None of these

5

$28 - {}^{-}3 =$

A 25
B ${}^{-}31$
C 31
D ${}^{-}25$
E None of these

10

${}^{-}5 - 15 =$

F ${}^{-}20$
G 10
H ${}^{-}10$
J 20
K None of these

Check your answers on page 64.

Lesson 14 Multiplication of Integers

When you multiply two integers, you follow the same steps as multiplying two whole numbers, but you also have to choose the correct sign. To find the sign, you need to remember two rules.

- If the signs of the two numbers are alike, the answer is positive.

$$6 \times 8 = 48 \qquad \quad ^-50 \times ^-7 = 350$$

- If the signs of the two numbers are different, the answer is negative.

$$12 \times ^-4 = ^-48 \qquad \quad ^-9 \times 7 = ^-63$$

Example   Multiply. $^-9 \times 4$

Step 1. Multiply the whole number part of the two integers together.

$$9 \times 4 = 36$$

Step 2. Determine the sign. Because one number is positive and the other number is negative, the answer is negative.

$$^-9 \times 4 = ^-36$$

Test Example

Multiply. Circle the answer.

1

$^-25 \times ^-5 =$

    A $^-125$

    B   120

    C   125

    D   None of these

1   C

$^-25 \times ^-5 = 125$

Multiply. Circle the answer.

1

$6 \times {}^-8 =$

- A ${}^-48$
- B 48
- C ${}^-42$
- D 48
- E None of these

2

${}^-4 \times {}^-15 =$

- F ${}^-60$
- G 60
- H ${}^-90$
- J 90
- K None of these

3

${}^-12 \times {}^-4 =$

- A ${}^-36$
- B 36
- C ${}^-54$
- D 54
- E None of these

4

$7 \times {}^-7 =$

- F ${}^-49$
- G ${}^-48$
- H 48
- J 49
- K None of these

5

${}^-6 \times 9 =$

- A 56
- B ${}^-56$
- C ${}^-54$
- D 54
- E None of these

6

$7 \times {}^-8 =$

- F 54
- G 56
- H ${}^-54$
- J ${}^-56$
- K None of these

7

${}^-5 \times 8 =$

- A 35
- B 40
- C ${}^-35$
- D ${}^-40$
- E None of these

8

${}^-7 \times {}^-4 =$

- F ${}^-21$
- G ${}^-28$
- H ${}^-35$
- J ${}^-42$
- K None of these

9

${}^-8 \times {}^-12 =$

- A ${}^-94$
- B 94
- C ${}^-96$
- D 96
- E None of these

10

$15 \times 15 =$

- F ${}^-225$
- G 225
- H ${}^-125$
- J 125
- K None of these

Check your answers on pages 64–65.

Lesson 15 Division of Integers

Dividing integers is almost the same as regular division, but you have pay attention to the signs. Here are two rules to remember.

- If the signs are the same, the answer is positive. $^-8 \div {}^-4 = 2$
- If the signs are different, the answer is negative. $8 \div {}^-4 = {}^-2$

Example Divide. $\dfrac{^-66}{^-11}$

Step 1. Write out the problem using the division bracket. Forget about the negative signs for now.

$$11\,\overline{)6\,6}$$

Step 2. Divide. The answer is $^+6$. When both numbers are negative, the answer is positive.

$$\begin{array}{r} 6 \\ 11\,\overline{)6\,6} \\ -6\,6 \\ \hline 0 \end{array}$$

$$\frac{^-66}{^-11} = 6$$

Test Example

Divide. Circle the answer.

1

$^-54 \div {}^-6 =$

A 9

B 8

C $^-9$

D $^-8$

E None of these

$$\begin{array}{l} \textbf{1} \quad \text{A} \quad ^-54 \div {}^-6 = \\ \qquad\qquad \begin{array}{r} 9 \\ 6\,\overline{)54} \\ -54 \\ \hline 0 \end{array} \end{array}$$

Divide. Circle the answer.

1

$^-72 \div ^-6 =$

A   10
B   12
C $^-12$
D $^-10$
E   None of these

6

$^-92 \div 4 =$

F   20
G $^-24$
H   24
J $^-20$
K   None of these

2

$^-96 \div ^-12 =$

F $^-6$
G $^-9$
H   6
J   9
K   None of these

7

$84 \div ^-7 =$

A   10
B $^-12$
C   12
D $^-10$
E   None of these

3

$96 \div ^-8 =$

A   12
B   14
C $^-12$
D $^-14$
E   None of these

8

$^-72 \div 18 =$

F $^-4$
G $^-6$
H   4
J   6
K   None of these

4

$80 \div ^-10 =$

F   8
G $^-10$
H $^-8$
J   10
K   None of these

9

$^-63 \div ^-3 =$

A   21
B   22
C $^-21$
D $^-20$
E   None of these

5

$^-85 \div ^-17 =$

A   6
B $^-6$
C   5
D $^-5$
E   None of these

10

$^-72 \div 24 =$

F   3
G $^-3$
H   2
J $^-2$
K   None of these

Check your answers on page 65.

1

$30 - {}^-5 =$

- **A** 25
- **B** 35
- **C** ⁻25
- **D** ⁻35
- **E** None of these

2

$^-80 \div {}^-5 =$

- **F** ⁻14
- **G** 14
- **H** ⁻16
- **J** 16
- **K** None of these

3

$^-9 + 4 =$

- **A** 13
- **B** ⁻5
- **C** ⁻7
- **D** ⁻11
- **E** None of these

4

$4 - {}^-9 =$

- **F** 13
- **G** ⁻13
- **H** ⁻5
- **J** 5
- **K** None of these

5

$^-99 \div {}^-11 =$

- **A** ⁻10
- **B** ⁻11
- **C** 10
- **D** 11
- **E** None of these

6

$7 + {}^-9 =$

- **F** ⁻16
- **G** 2
- **H** ⁻2
- **J** 16
- **K** None of these

7

$^-65 \div {}^-5 =$

- **A** ⁻13
- **B** 12
- **C** ⁻12
- **D** 13
- **E** None of these

8

$^-4 - 18 =$

- **F** ⁻14
- **G** 22
- **H** 14
- **J** ⁻22
- **K** None of these

9

$5 \times {}^-6 =$

- **A** ⁻1
- **B** 1
- **C** ⁻30
- **D** 30
- **E** None of these

10

$8 \times {}^-4 =$

- **F** ⁻2
- **G** 32
- **H** ⁻32
- **J** 2
- **K** None of these

11			16		
$60 \div {}^-15 =$	**A**	${}^-4$	${}^-7 - 4 =$	**F**	${}^-11$
	B	${}^-5$		**G**	11
	C	4		**H**	${}^-3$
	D	5		**J**	3
	E	None of these		**K**	None of these

12			17		
$5 + {}^-4 =$	**F**	0	$6 + {}^-10 =$	**A**	${}^-4$
	G	${}^-9$		**B**	${}^-16$
	H	9		**C**	4
	J	${}^-1$		**D**	16
	K	None of these		**E**	None of these

13			18		
$26 - {}^-3 =$	**A**	${}^-23$	$84 \div {}^-21 =$	**F**	${}^-4$
	B	29		**G**	${}^-2$
	C	${}^-29$		**H**	4
	D	23		**J**	2
	E	None of these		**K**	None of these

14			19		
${}^-76 \div 4 =$	**F**	${}^-14$	${}^-3 + 11 =$	**A**	${}^-4$
	G	14		**B**	4
	H	${}^-18$		**C**	8
	J	18		**D**	14
	K	None of these		**E**	None of these

15			20		
${}^-6 + 8 =$	**A**	${}^-4$	${}^-3 - 11 =$	**F**	${}^-8$
	B	14		**G**	${}^-14$
	C	${}^-8$		**H**	8
	D	2		**J**	14
	E	None of these		**K**	None of these

Check your answers on page 65.

Lesson 16 · Percents—Finding the Part

Being able to use percents can be useful when figuring discounts or sales tax at the store. A percent can be written as a fraction or a decimal. The "%," or *percent,* means "per (out of) cent (100) parts." If you want to figure out what 80% of 50 is, you can change the problem into a decimal multiplication problem. 80% is the same as $\frac{80}{100}$ or 0.80, or more simply, 0.8. The word "of" means you are going to multiply.

Example   Multiply. 80% of 50 =

Step 1. Every percent problem has three elements: the whole, the percent, and the part. Find the whole, the percent, and the part.

- The **percent** is easy to find because it is usually a number followed by a percent sign, "%." In this example, the percent is *80%*.
- The **whole** is the whole amount. The whole represents 100%. The whole usually follows the word *of*. In this example, the whole is *50*.
- The **part** is part of the whole amount. The part usually follows or comes before the equal sign, or the word *is*. In this example, the part follows the "=" sign. Because "the part" is unknown, that's what we'll be looking for.

80% **(the percent)** of 50 **(the whole)** = _____ **(the part)**

Step 2. Rewrite the problem, changing the percent to a decimal and the "of" to a multiplication sign.
$$0.8 \times 50 =$$

Step 3. Multiply using what you already know about multiplying decimals. Remember to count the number of decimal places in the numbers you are multiplying. Because 8 has one decimal place, begin from the right of the decimal and count one place to the left. 40.0 is "the part."

$$.8 \times 50 = 50$$
$$\frac{\times\ .8}{40.0}$$

80% of 50 = 40.0

Example   Multiply. 70% of $6.20 =

Step 1. Label the percent, the whole, and the part in the problem.

70% **(the percent)** of $6.20 **(the whole)** = _____ **(the part)**

Step 2. Rewrite the problem. Change the percent to a decimal and the "of" to a multiplication sign. Drop the 0 on the end of $6.20 because it's just a placeholder. Drop the $ for now.

0.70 of $6.20 is the same as **0.7 × 6.2**

Step 3. Set up the problem vertically to make multiplication easier. Multiply, using what you already know about multiplying decimals. Because there is one decimal place in 6.2 and one in 0.7, place the decimal point two places from the right of the last number in the answer.

Hint

When you are finding a percentage of a dollar amount, remember to count the decimal places of both numbers.

$$0.7 \times 6.2 = \begin{array}{r} \overset{1}{6.2} \\ \times\ 0.7 \\ \hline 4.34 \end{array}$$

Rewrite the answer in dollar format just like the problem: $4.34 is "the part."
70% of $6.20 = $4.34

Test Example

Multiply. Circle the answer.

1

40% of 61 =

A   244.0

B   24.4

C   0.244

D   2.44

E   None of these

1   **B**   40% of 61 = 0.4 × 61 =
$$\begin{array}{r} 61 \\ \times\ 0.4 \\ \hline 24.4 \end{array}$$

Read the question. Circle the answer.

1

50% of $9.00 =

A $1.82

B $18.20

C $4.50

D $45.00

E None of these

2

70% of 54 =

F 0.378

G 3.78

H 378.0

J 37.8

K None of these

3

40% of 90 =

A 36.0

B 3.6

C 360.0

D 0.36

E None of these

4

100% of 76 =

F 7.6

G 76

H 0.76

J .760

K None of these

5

80% of $10 =

A $80

B $0.80

C $16.00

D $8.00

E None of these

6

20% of 50 =

F 100.0

G 1.0

H 0.10

J 10.0

K None of these

7

60% of 100 =

A 60

B 6

C 600

D 0.6

E None of these

8

100% of 83 =

F 83.0

G 830.0

H 8.3

J 0.83

K None of these

9

90% of 80 =

A 810.0

B 81.0

C 0.81

D 8.1

E None of these

10

1% of 72 =

F 72

G 720

H 7.2

J 0.72

K None of these

Check your answers on pages 65–66.

On the TABE you sometimes have to find the "whole" or the "percent" instead of finding the "part". In problems where you have to find a whole, there will be a ☐ in the problem.

Example Solve. 90% of ☐ = 36

Step 1. Label the percent, the whole, and the part.

90% **(the percent)** of ☐ **(the whole)** =

36 **(the part)**

In this problem, we know the percent and the part, so we'll be looking for the whole.

Step 2. Rewrite the problem. Change the percent to a decimal and the "of" to a multiplication sign. Before you can solve the problem, you'll need to get all the numbers on one side of the "=" and the ☐ on the other.

$$0.9 \times \square = 36$$

Step 3. Division and multiplication are opposite operations, which means division undoes multiplication. Divide both sides by 0.9. The multiplication problem now becomes a division problem.

$$\square = 36 \div 0.9$$

Step 4. Now rewrite the problem using the division bracket. Divide, using what you already know about dividing decimals. Remember to place the decimal point above the decimal in the division bracket. Because we don't normally express a whole number with a decimal point, you can drop the decimal point in the answer. 40 is "the whole."

$$
\begin{array}{r}
40. \\
9.\overline{)360.} \\
-36 \\
\hline
00
\end{array}
$$

90% of ☐40 = 36.

Example Solve. **What percent of 40 is 56?**

Step 1. Label the percent, the whole, and the part in the problem.

the whole

What percent of ☐40 is ⟨56⟩?

the percent   the part

In this problem, we know the whole and the part, so we're looking for the percent.

Step 2. Rewrite the problem. Change "of" to a multiplication sign and "is" to an equal sign. Change "what percent" to ☐ %.

☐ % × 40 = 56

Step 3. Move the numbers around so that the □ is on one side of the "=" sign and the numbers are on the other. Change the operation sign to the opposite operation of multiplication, which is division.

$$\square\% = 56 \div 40$$

Step 4. Rewrite the problem, using the division bracket. Divide, using what you already know about dividing decimals. Remember to place the decimal point above the decimal in the division bracket.

$$
\begin{array}{r}
1.4 \\
40\overline{)56.0} \\
-40 \\
\hline
16\,0 \\
-16\,0 \\
\hline
0
\end{array}
$$

Step 5. Remember that you're looking for a percent. Because percent means "out of 100," multiply the answer by 100 to get a percent. $1.4 \times 100 = 140.0$. You can drop the decimal point and the zero after it. Add the "%" sign to the answer. 140 is "the percent."

$$
\begin{array}{r}
100 \\
\times\ \ 1.4 \\
\hline
400 \\
+\ 1000 \\
\hline
140.0
\end{array}
$$

56 is 140% of 40.

Test Example

Solve. Circle the answer.

1

60% of □ = 84

    A 710

    B 14

    C 140

    D 71

    E None of these

TABE Strategy

Read each problem carefully to find out what you are looking for.

1 **C** 60% of □ = 84 → .6 × □ = 84 → 84 ÷ .6 =

$$
\begin{array}{r}
140 \\
6\overline{)840} \\
-6 \\
\hline
24 \\
-24 \\
\hline
00
\end{array}
$$

Read the question. Circle the answer.

1

40% of □ = 32

A   8.0

B 80.0

C 1.28

D 128.0

E None of these

2

What percent of 100 is 70?

F 7%

G 70%

H 14%

J 10%

K None of these

3

24% of □ = 72

A 3,400

B   340

C 3,000

D   300

E None of these

4

20% of □ = 54

F   27

G 207

H 370

J   37

K None of these

5

What percent of 90 is 99?

A 11%

B 90%

C 110%

D   9%

E None of these

6

13% of □ = 91

F   700

G 1,400

H   140

J 7,000

K None of these

7

What percent of 400 is 80?

A 2%

B 5%

C 20%

D 50%

E None of these

8

70% of □ = 70

F 70

G 110

H 30

J   7

K None of these

Check your answers on page 66.

1

100% of $8.50 =

A $850
B $8.50
C $0.85
D $85.00
E   None of these

2

What percent of 300 is 90?

F   20%
G   3%
H   33%
J   60%
K   None of these

3

80% of ☐ = 56

A   70.0
B   448.0
C   0.7
D   4.48
E   None of these

4

50% of 40 =

F   0.2
G   2.0
H   200.0
J   20.0
K   None of these

5

What percent of 60 is 96?

A   160%
B   620%
C   62%
D   16%
E   None of these

6

30% of 28 =

F   840.0
G   84.0
H   8.4
J   0.84
K   None of these

7

15% of ☐ = 75

A   5,000
B   200
C   500
D   2,000
E   None of these

8

90% of $1.70 =

F $1.53
G $15.30
H $18.80
J $1.88
K   None of these

9

70% of □ = 91

A 76
B 13
C 760
D 130
E None of these

10

50% of □ = 45

F 0.9
G 225.0
H 90.0
J 2.25
K None of these

11

80% of 20 =

A 0.16
B 16.0
C 160.0
D 1.6
E None of these

12

100% of 43 =

F 43.0
G 430.0
H 4.3
J 0.43
K None of these

13

What percent of 50 is 65?

A 13%
B 130%
C 760%
D 76%
E None of these

14

1% of 3.70 =

F 3.70
G 0.37
H 0.037
J 37
K None of these

15

11% of □ = 88

A 880
B 8000
C 125
D 1250
E None of these

16

80% of 100 =

F 800
G 18
H 100
J 80
K None of these

17

10% of 60 =

A 60.0
B 6.0
C 0.6
D 600.0
E None of these

18

20% of □ = 12

F 0.6
G 240.0
H 2.4
J 60.0
K None of these

Check your answers on pages 66–67.

The Math Computation Assessment is identical to the actual TABE in format and length. It will give you an idea of what the real test is like. Allow yourself 15 minutes to complete this assessment. Check your answers on pages 67–68.

Sample A

Add.

$42 + 10 =$

A 32
B 42
C 22
D 52
E None of these

1

$$\begin{array}{r} 64 \\ \times\ 9 \end{array}$$

A 606
B 585
C 576
D 546
E None of these

2

$276 \div 6 =$

F 45
G 36
H 46
J 41
K None of these

3

$491 \times 4 =$

A 1,624
B 1,924
C 1,664
D 1,946
E None of these

4

$4\overline{)92}$

F 20
G 23
H 24
J 22
K None of these

5

$$\begin{array}{r} 4.63 \\ -\ 4.19 \end{array}$$

A 0.56
B 0.43
C 0.44
D 0.54
E None of these

6

$$\begin{array}{r} 6.2 \\ +\ 2.4 \end{array}$$

F 8.2
G 8.06
H 8.6
J 0.86
K None of these

7

$90 \div 15 =$

A 5
B 4
C 8
D 10
E None of these

8

$$\begin{array}{r} 563 \\ \times\ \ 70 \\ \hline \end{array}$$

F 39,410
G 35,210
H 35,410
J 39,400
K None of these

9

$33 \div 4 =$

A 18 R1
B 8
C 9 R3
D 8 R1
E None of these

10

$46 \times 37 =$

F 1,602
G 1,662
H 1,702
J 1,562
K None of these

11

$^-96 \div\ ^-16 =$

A $^-6$
B 6
C $^-10$
D 10
E None of these

12

$$\begin{array}{r} 8.421 \\ +\ 0.363 \\ \hline \end{array}$$

F 12.024
G 8.894
H 12.24
J 8.784
K None of these

13

$\dfrac{4}{5} \times \dfrac{8}{1} =$

A $6\dfrac{2}{5}$
B $\dfrac{1}{10}$
C $2\dfrac{2}{5}$
D $6\dfrac{1}{5}$
E None of these

14

20% of $5.40 =

F $1.80
G $27.00
H $2.70
J $10.80
K None of these

15

40% of $\square$ = 84

A 21
B 210
C 47
D 470
E None of these

16

$\dfrac{7}{8} - \dfrac{1}{8} =$

F $\dfrac{7}{8}$
G $\dfrac{3}{4}$
H $\dfrac{1}{2}$
J $\dfrac{5}{8}$
K None of these

17

50% of 57 =

A 28.5
B 2.85
C 285.0
D 0.285
E None of these

Performance Assessment

18

$\dfrac{8}{13} + \dfrac{5}{13} =$

    F $\dfrac{12}{13}$

    G $1\dfrac{1}{6}$

    H   1

    J $\dfrac{1}{2}$

    K   None of these

19

$5\dfrac{3}{4} + 8\dfrac{4}{5} =$

    A $5\dfrac{4}{5}$

    B $8\dfrac{16}{20}$

    C $\dfrac{20}{31}$

    D $14\dfrac{11}{20}$

    E   None of these

20

$6 + {}^{-}3 =$

    F   9

    G   3

    H ${}^{-}9$

    J ${}^{-}3$

    K   None of these

21

${}^{-}8 \times {}^{-}6 =$

    A ${}^{-}48$

    B ${}^{-}54$

    C   48

    D   54

    E   None of these

22

$\begin{array}{r} 2.6 \\ \times\ 3.1 \\ \hline \end{array}$

    F   7.106

    G   7

    H   2.6

    J   8.06

    K   None of these

23

What percent of 40 is 96?

    A   41%

    B   24%

    C   140%

    D   410%

    E   None of these

24

$0.82\overline{)984}$

    F   1,200.0

    G   1.2

    H   12.0

    J   120.0

    K   None of these

25

${}^{-}6 - 14 =$

    A ${}^{-}8$

    B ${}^{-}20$

    C   20

    D   8

    E   None of these

STOP ✳

Lesson 1 Multiplication of Whole Numbers—Regrouping (page 9)

1. B
$$\begin{array}{r} \overset{1}{}43 \\ \times\quad 5 \\ \hline 215 \end{array}$$

2. F
$$\begin{array}{r} \overset{2}{}327 \\ \times\quad 3 \\ \hline 981 \end{array}$$

3. D
$$\begin{array}{r} \overset{2}{}631 \\ \times\quad 73 \\ \hline 1893 \\ +\ 44170 \\ \hline 46{,}063 \end{array}$$

4. G
$$\begin{array}{r} \overset{11}{}5331 \\ \times\quad 24 \\ \hline 21324 \\ +\ 106620 \\ \hline 127{,}944 \end{array}$$

5. A
$$\begin{array}{r} \overset{2}{}75 \\ \times\quad 4 \\ \hline 300 \end{array}$$

6. K
$$\begin{array}{r} \overset{1}{\overset{1}{}}63 \\ \times\quad 54 \\ \hline \overset{1}{}252 \\ +\ 3150 \\ \hline 3{,}402 \end{array}$$

7. D
$$\begin{array}{r} \overset{3}{}508 \\ \times\quad 4 \\ \hline 2{,}032 \end{array}$$

8. J
$$\begin{array}{r} \overset{24}{}649 \\ \times\quad 500 \\ \hline 324{,}500 \end{array}$$

9. C
$$\begin{array}{r} \overset{2}{}74 \\ \times\quad 52 \\ \hline 148 \\ +\ 3700 \\ \hline 3{,}848 \end{array}$$

10. G
$$\begin{array}{r} \overset{41}{}762 \\ \times\quad 8 \\ \hline 6{,}096 \end{array}$$

Lesson 2 Division of Whole Numbers—No Remainder (page 11)

1. A
$$\begin{array}{r} 58 \\ 4\overline{)232} \\ -20 \\ \hline 32 \\ -32 \\ \hline 0 \end{array}$$

2. H
$$\begin{array}{r} 17 \\ 5\overline{)85} \\ -5 \\ \hline 35 \\ -35 \\ \hline 0 \end{array}$$

3. C
$$\begin{array}{r} 3 \\ 19\overline{)57} \\ -57 \\ \hline 0 \end{array}$$

4. F
$$\begin{array}{r} 1638 \\ 4\overline{)6552} \\ -4 \\ \hline 25 \\ -24 \\ \hline 15 \\ -12 \\ \hline 32 \\ -32 \\ \hline 0 \end{array}$$

5. D
$$\begin{array}{r} 26 \\ 5\overline{)130} \\ -10 \\ \hline 30 \\ -30 \\ \hline 0 \end{array}$$

6. K
$$\begin{array}{r} 30 \\ 17\overline{)510} \\ -51 \\ \hline 00 \end{array}$$

7. A
$$\begin{array}{r} 93 \\ 4\overline{)372} \\ -36 \\ \hline 12 \\ -12 \\ \hline 0 \end{array}$$

8. H
$$\begin{array}{r} 63 \\ 6\overline{)378} \\ -36 \\ \hline 18 \\ -18 \\ \hline 0 \end{array}$$

9. A
$$\begin{array}{r} 25 \\ 3\overline{)75} \\ -6 \\ \hline 15 \\ -15 \\ \hline 0 \end{array}$$

10. H
$$\begin{array}{r} 139 \\ 5\overline{)695} \\ -5 \\ \hline 19 \\ -15 \\ \hline 45 \\ -45 \\ \hline 0 \end{array}$$

Lesson 3 Division of Whole Numbers—Remainder (page 13)

1. C
$$\begin{array}{r} 7\ R2 \\ 9\overline{)65} \\ -63 \\ \hline 2 \end{array}$$

2. K
$$\begin{array}{r} 14\ R3 \\ 6\overline{)87} \\ -6 \\ \hline 27 \\ -24 \\ \hline 3 \end{array}$$

3. C
$$\begin{array}{r} 35\ R1 \\ 7\overline{)246} \\ -21 \\ \hline 36 \\ -35 \\ \hline 1 \end{array}$$

4. F
```
      42 R1
  14)589
   − 56
     29
    − 28
      1
```

5. D
```
      28 R11
  12)347
   − 24
    107
    − 96
     11
```

6. H
```
     9 R5
  6)59
  − 54
     5
```

7. A
```
     8 R4
     5 10
  7)6 0
  − 56
     4
```

8. G
```
     26 R6
  7)188
  − 14
    48
   − 42
     6
```

9. B
```
     15 R3
  5)78
  − 5
    28
   − 25
     3
```

10. F
```
     51 R5
  8)413
  − 40
    13
   − 8
     5
```

TABE Review: Multiplication and Division of Whole Numbers (pages 14–15)

1. E
```
    108
  3)324
  − 3
    024
   − 24
     0
```
[Division of Whole Numbers—No Remainder]

2. H
```
     2
    94
  × 17
   658
  + 940
  1,598
```
[Multiplication of Whole Numbers—Regrouping]

3. B
```
    7 R2
  5)37
  − 35
     2
```
[Division of Whole Numbers—Remainder]

4. H
```
    1 1
    556
  ×   2
  1,112
```
[Multiplication of Whole Numbers—Regrouping]

5. B
```
     2 1
    742
  ×  15
     1
   3710
  + 7420
  11,130
```
[Multiplication of Whole Numbers—Regrouping]

6. J
```
      8
  13)104
   − 104
     00
    − 00
      0
```
[Division of Whole Numbers—No Remainder]

7. D
```
     3
     2
    95
  ×  65
     1
   475
  + 5700
  6,175
```
[Multiplication of Whole Numbers—Regrouping]

8. G
```
    2584
  3)7752
  − 6
    17
   − 15
    25
   − 24
    12
   − 12
     0
```
[Division of Whole Numbers—No Remainder]

9. E
```
     32 R1
  2)65
  − 6
    5
  − 4
    1
```
[Division of Whole Numbers—Remainder]

10. F
```
     24 R2
  4)98
  − 8
    18
  − 16
    2
```
[Division of Whole Numbers—Remainder]

11. A
```
       22
       11
     9167
  ×    42
     111
    18334
  + 366680
  385,014
```
[Multiplication of Whole Numbers—Regrouping]

12. K
```
     56
  7)392
  − 35
    42
  − 42
     0
```
[Division of Whole Numbers—No Remainder]

13. D
```
     5
  17)85
   − 85
     0
```
[Division of Whole Numbers—No Remainder]

14. H
```
     5
    909
  ×   6
  5,454
```
[Multiplication of Whole Numbers—Regrouping]

15. D
```
    18 R3
  4)75
  − 4
    35
  − 32
    3
```
[Division of Whole Numbers—Remainder]

16. G
```
      2
    931
  ×  307
    1
   6517
  +.279300
  285,817
```
[Multiplication of Whole Numbers—Regrouping]

17. A
```
     8 R7
     6 11
  8)7 1
  − 64
     7
```
[Division of Whole Numbers—Remainder]

18. F
$$\begin{array}{r} 13 \\ 6\overline{)78} \\ -6 \\ \hline 18 \\ -18 \\ \hline 0 \end{array}$$
[Division of Whole Numbers—No Remainder]

Lesson 4 Addition of Decimals (page 17)

1. B
$$\begin{array}{r} 7.342 \\ + 2.526 \\ \hline 9.868 \end{array}$$

2. K
$$\begin{array}{r} 7.46 \\ + 0.23 \\ \hline 7.69 \end{array}$$

3. B
$$\begin{array}{r} {}^{1\,1} \\ 4.35 \\ + 0.78 \\ \hline 5.13 \end{array}$$

4. F
$$\begin{array}{r} 7.03 \\ + 4.10 \\ \hline 11.13 \end{array}$$

5. E
$$\begin{array}{r} {}^{1\,1\,1} \\ 237.943 \\ + 46.085 \\ \hline 284.028 \end{array}$$

6. G
$$\begin{array}{r} {}^{1\,1} \\ 3.75 \\ + 0.66 \\ \hline 4.41 \end{array}$$

7. D
$$\begin{array}{r} {}^{1\,1} \\ 6.749 \\ + 4.610 \\ \hline 11.359 \end{array}$$

8. H
$$\begin{array}{r} 9.03 \\ + 4.20 \\ \hline 13.23 \end{array}$$

9. D
$$\begin{array}{r} 4.1 \\ + 1.8 \\ \hline 5.9 \end{array}$$

10. K
$$\begin{array}{r} {}^{1\,1} \\ 0.84 \\ + 2.39 \\ \hline 3.23 \end{array}$$

Lesson 5 Subtraction of Decimals (page 19)

1. C
$$\begin{array}{r} {}^{5\ \,9\,9\,10} \\ 36.000 \\ - 0.024 \\ \hline 35.976 \end{array}$$

2. F
$$\begin{array}{r} {}^{6\ \,9\,14} \\ 7.04 \\ - 0.39 \\ \hline 6.65 \end{array}$$

3. C
$$\begin{array}{r} {}^{5\ \,9\,10} \\ 6.00 \\ - 1.68 \\ \hline 4.32 \end{array}$$

4. F
$$\begin{array}{r} {}^{8\,13} \\ 6.93 \\ - 6.48 \\ \hline 0.45 \end{array}$$

5. E
$$\begin{array}{r} {}^{3\,13} \\ 8.43 \\ - 6.25 \\ \hline 2.18 \end{array}$$

6. H
$$\begin{array}{r} {}^{8\ \,9\,12} \\ 9.02 \\ - 0.54 \\ \hline 8.48 \end{array}$$

7. D
$$\begin{array}{r} {}^{5\ \,9\,10} \\ 6.008 \\ - 0.292 \\ \hline 5.716 \end{array}$$

8. J
$$\begin{array}{r} {}^{4\,11} \\ 3.51 \\ - 3.27 \\ \hline 0.24 \end{array}$$

9. E
$$\begin{array}{r} {}^{1\ \,9\,9\,10} \\ 52.000 \\ - 0.058 \\ \hline 51.942 \end{array}$$

10. G
$$\begin{array}{r} {}^{4\,13} \\ 4.532 \\ - 2.151 \\ \hline 2.381 \end{array}$$

Lesson 6 Multiplication of Decimals (page 21)

1. D
$$\begin{array}{r} {}^{2} \\ 0.3 \\ \times \ 7 \\ \hline 2.1 \end{array}$$

2. J
$$\begin{array}{r} {}^{2} \\ 0.8 \\ \times \ 3.0 \\ \hline 00 \\ + \ 2\,40 \\ \hline 2.40 \end{array}$$

3. D
$$\begin{array}{r} {}^{2} \\ 7.2 \\ \times \ 1.3 \\ \hline 2\,16 \\ + \ 7\,20 \\ \hline 9.36 \end{array}$$

4. G
$$\begin{array}{r} 3.1 \\ \times \ 4.2 \\ \hline {}^{1}\,62 \\ + \ 12\,40 \\ \hline 13.02 \end{array}$$

5. E
$$\begin{array}{r} 0.7 \\ \times \ 0.5 \\ \hline 35 \\ + \ 0\,00 \\ \hline 0.35 \end{array}$$

6. H
$$\begin{array}{r} {}^{1} \\ 5.2 \\ \times \ 8.0 \\ \hline 00 \\ + \ 41\,60 \\ \hline 41.60 \end{array}$$

7. A
$$\begin{array}{r} {}^{3} \\ 6.8 \\ \times \ 4.1 \\ \hline 68 \\ + \ 27\,20 \\ \hline 27.88 \end{array}$$

8. G
$$\begin{array}{r} 8 \\ \times 0.3 \\ \hline 2.4 \end{array}$$

9. C
$$\begin{array}{r} {}^{1} \\ 5.3 \\ \times \ 2.1 \\ \hline {}^{1}\,53 \\ + \ 10\,60 \\ \hline 11.13 \end{array}$$

10. K
$$\begin{array}{r} 6.3 \\ \times \ 1.2 \\ \hline 1\,26 \\ + \ 6\,30 \\ \hline 7.56 \end{array}$$

1. E
```
     .005
8)0.040
 − 40
    0
```

2. J
```
    1200
21)25200
 − 21
   42
 − 42
    0
```

3. C
```
    0.19875
16)3.18000
 − 16
   158
 − 144
   140
 − 128
   120
 − 112
    80
  − 80
     0
```

4. G
```
    0.1208
25)3.0200
 − 2 5
   52
 − 50
   200
 − 200
     0
```

5. A
```
    3000
026)78000
  − 78
    0000
  − 000
      0
```

6. K
```
    18300
004)73200
  − 4
   33
 − 32
   12
 − 12
   000
 − 000
     0
```

7. B
```
    2100
039)81900
  − 78
   39
 − 39
   000
 − 000
     0
```

8. H
```
    0.028
60)1.680
 − 1 20
   480
 − 480
     0
```

9. A
```
    0.242
15)3.630
 − 3 0
   63
 − 60
   30
 − 30
    0
```

10. K
```
    150
074)11100
  − 74
   370
 − 370
    00
  − 00
     0
```

1. A
```
   3.7    [Addition of
 + 2.2      Decimals]
   5.9
```

2. H
```
    8400
09)75600   [Division of
 − 72       Decimals]
   36
 − 36
    0
```

3. D
```
   57.000   [Subtraction of
 − 0.039     Decimals]
   56.961
```

4. F
```
   6.05   [Addition of
 + 0.93     Decimals]
   6.98
```

5. B
```
     6.5
 ×   3.3
     1 95   [Multiplication
 + 19 50     of Decimals]
    21.45
```

6. K
```
    0.0785
20)1.5700     [Division of
 − 1 40        Decimals]
   170
 − 160
   100
 − 100
     0
```

7. B
```
   5.74   [Subtraction of
 − 5.36     Decimals]
   0.38
```

8. K
```
   9.751   [Addition of
 + 0.592     Decimals]
   10.343
```

9. D
```
    0.13
72)9.36   [Division of
 − 7 2      Decimals]
   2 16
 − 2 16
     0
```

10. G
```
     7.6   [Multiplication of
 ×    4      Decimals]
    30.4
```

11. B
```
    5.000   [Subtraction of
 − 0.450     Decimals]
   4.550
```

12. H
```
     387.5
064)24800.0   [Division
  − 192        of
    560        Decimals]
  − 512
    480
  − 448
    320
  − 320
      0
```

13. C $\overset{1}{}$
$$\begin{array}{r} 8.9 \\ + \ 4.3 \\ \hline 13.2 \end{array}$$
[Addition of Decimals]

14. F $\overset{31}{}$
$$\begin{array}{r} 4.2 \\ \times \ \ 8 \\ \hline 33.6 \end{array}$$
[Multiplication of Decimals]

15. D
$$\begin{array}{r} 8.701 \\ + \ 3.041 \\ \hline 11.742 \end{array}$$
[Addition of Decimals]

16. F $\overset{5}{\overset{1}{}}$
$$\begin{array}{r} 7.1 \\ \times \ \ 8.2 \\ \hline 1\ 42 \\ + \ 56\ 80 \\ \hline 58.22 \end{array}$$
[Multiplication of Decimals]

17. D
$$\begin{array}{r} 1.06 \\ 9\overline{)9.54} \\ -\ 9 \ \ \ \\ \hline 05 \\ -\ 0 \ \\ \hline 54 \\ -\ 54 \\ \hline 0 \end{array}$$
[Division of Decimals]

18. K $\overset{7\ 914}{}$
$$\begin{array}{r} 8.0\cancel{4} \\ -\ 0.28 \\ \hline 7.76 \end{array}$$
[Subtraction of Decimals]

Lesson 8 Addition of Fractions (page 28)

1. A $\dfrac{3}{14} + \dfrac{8}{14} = \dfrac{11}{14}$

2. J $\dfrac{3}{4} + \dfrac{2}{8} =$

$\dfrac{6}{8} + \dfrac{2}{8} = \dfrac{8}{8} = 1$

3. B $\dfrac{11}{18} + \dfrac{7}{18} = \dfrac{18}{18} = 1$

4. H $\dfrac{8}{27} + \dfrac{10}{27} = \dfrac{18}{27} = \dfrac{2}{3}$

5. E $\dfrac{2}{3} + \dfrac{5}{6} =$

$\dfrac{4}{6} + \dfrac{5}{6} = \dfrac{9}{6} =$

$1\dfrac{3}{6} = 1\dfrac{1}{2}$

---

6. F $6\dfrac{4}{5} + 5\dfrac{2}{4} =$

$6\dfrac{16}{20} + 5\dfrac{10}{20} = 11\dfrac{26}{20} =$

$12\dfrac{6}{20} = 12\dfrac{3}{10}$

7. D $\dfrac{9}{19} + \dfrac{5}{19} = \dfrac{14}{19}$

8. G $2\dfrac{95}{100} + 3\dfrac{3}{10} =$

$2\dfrac{95}{100} + 3\dfrac{30}{100} =$

$5\dfrac{125}{100} = 6\dfrac{25}{100} = 6\dfrac{1}{4}$

Lesson 9 Subtraction of Fractions (page 31)

1. D $1 - \dfrac{5}{9} = \dfrac{9}{9} - \dfrac{5}{9} = \dfrac{4}{9}$

2. J $7\dfrac{4}{5} - 1\dfrac{2}{10} = 7\dfrac{4}{5} - 1\dfrac{1}{5} = 6\dfrac{3}{5}$

3. E $\dfrac{4}{5} - \dfrac{2}{5} = \dfrac{2}{5}$

4. G $8\dfrac{3}{4} - 6\dfrac{1}{2} = 8\dfrac{3}{4} - 6\dfrac{2}{4} = 2\dfrac{1}{4}$

5. B $\dfrac{4}{9} - \dfrac{1}{3} = \dfrac{4}{9} - \dfrac{3}{9} = \dfrac{1}{9}$

6. G $3 - 2\dfrac{2}{6} = \dfrac{18}{6} - \dfrac{14}{6} = \dfrac{4}{6} = \dfrac{2}{3}$

7. C $7 - 1\dfrac{2}{7} = \dfrac{49}{7} - \dfrac{9}{7} = \dfrac{40}{7} = 5\dfrac{5}{7}$

8. H $4\dfrac{5}{8} - 2\dfrac{3}{8} = 2\dfrac{2}{8} = 2\dfrac{1}{4}$

Lesson 10 Multiplication of Fractions (page 33)

1. A $\dfrac{2}{5} \times \dfrac{2}{3} = \dfrac{4}{15}$

2. K $\dfrac{5}{9} \times \dfrac{3}{4} = \dfrac{15}{36} = \dfrac{5}{12}$

3. C $\dfrac{5}{6} \times \dfrac{1}{2} = \dfrac{5}{12}$

---

4. F $\dfrac{2}{3} \times \dfrac{5}{1} = \dfrac{10}{3} = 3\dfrac{1}{3}$

5. B $\dfrac{3}{8} \times \dfrac{5}{8} = \dfrac{15}{64}$

6. K $\dfrac{3}{4} \times \dfrac{2}{9} = \dfrac{6}{36} = \dfrac{1}{6}$

7. C $\dfrac{1}{2} \times \dfrac{1}{6} = \dfrac{1}{12}$

8. H $\dfrac{4}{5} \times \dfrac{2}{1} = \dfrac{8}{5} = 1\dfrac{3}{5}$

Lesson 11 Division of Fractions (page 35)

1. C $2\dfrac{5}{6} \div 4 = \dfrac{17}{6} \times \dfrac{1}{4} = \dfrac{17}{24}$

2. H $\dfrac{3}{4} \div \dfrac{1}{2} = \dfrac{3}{4} \times \dfrac{2}{1} = \dfrac{6}{4} =$

$\dfrac{3}{2} = 1\dfrac{1}{2}$

3. D $3\dfrac{2}{3} \div 3 = \dfrac{11}{3} \times \dfrac{1}{3} = \dfrac{11}{9} = 1\dfrac{2}{9}$

4. F $4\dfrac{2}{7} \div 5 = \dfrac{30}{7} \times \dfrac{1}{5} = \dfrac{30}{35} = \dfrac{6}{7}$

5. E $\dfrac{2}{3} \div \dfrac{5}{6} = \dfrac{2}{3} \times \dfrac{6}{5} = \dfrac{12}{15} = \dfrac{4}{5}$

6. F $\dfrac{4}{9} \div 5 = \dfrac{4}{9} \times \dfrac{1}{5} = \dfrac{4}{45}$

7. C $\dfrac{2}{7} \div \dfrac{3}{4} = \dfrac{2}{7} \times \dfrac{4}{3} = \dfrac{8}{21}$

8. J $\dfrac{1}{5} \div \dfrac{2}{3} = \dfrac{1}{5} \times \dfrac{3}{2} = \dfrac{3}{10}$

TABE Review: Fractions (pages 36–37)

1. C $8\dfrac{4}{9} - 7\dfrac{2}{9} = 1\dfrac{2}{9}$

[Subtraction of Fractions]

2. K $\dfrac{3}{11} + \dfrac{7}{11} = \dfrac{10}{11}$

[Addition of Fractions]

3. A $\dfrac{2}{9} \div \dfrac{1}{3} = \dfrac{2}{9} \times \dfrac{3}{1} = \dfrac{6}{9} = \dfrac{2}{3}$

[Division of Fractions]

4. J $\dfrac{5}{6} \times \dfrac{2}{3} = \dfrac{10}{18} = \dfrac{5}{9}$

[Multiplication of Fractions]

5. C $\dfrac{6}{8} - \dfrac{1}{4} = \dfrac{3}{4} - \dfrac{1}{4} = \dfrac{2}{4} = \dfrac{1}{2}$

[Subtraction of Fractions]

6. K $\dfrac{3}{4} \div \dfrac{5}{6} = \dfrac{3}{4} \times \dfrac{6}{5} = \dfrac{18}{20} = \dfrac{9}{10}$

[Division of Fractions]

7. D $\dfrac{2}{7} \times \dfrac{1}{4} = \dfrac{2}{28} = \dfrac{1}{14}$

[Multiplication of Fractions]

8. H $3\dfrac{55}{100} + 4\dfrac{8}{10} =$

$3\dfrac{55}{100} + 4\dfrac{80}{100} =$

$7\dfrac{135}{100} = 8\dfrac{35}{100} = 8\dfrac{7}{20}$

[Addition of Fractions]

9. D $4 - 2\dfrac{1}{6} = \dfrac{24}{6} - \dfrac{13}{6} =$

$\dfrac{11}{6} = 1\dfrac{5}{6}$

[Subtraction of Fractions]

10. H $\dfrac{9}{22} + \dfrac{13}{22} = \dfrac{22}{22} = 1$

[Addition of Fractions]

11. B $3\dfrac{3}{5} \div 2 = \dfrac{18}{5} \times \dfrac{1}{2} = \dfrac{18}{10} =$

$1\dfrac{8}{10} = 1\dfrac{4}{5}$

[Division of Fractions]

12. F $4\dfrac{1}{4} + 5\dfrac{2}{5} =$

$4\dfrac{5}{20} + 5\dfrac{8}{20} = 9\dfrac{13}{20}$

[Addition of Fractions]

13. E $9 - 8\dfrac{1}{6} = \dfrac{54}{6} - \dfrac{49}{6} = \dfrac{5}{6}$

[Subtraction of Fractions]

14. H $2\dfrac{7}{25} + 1\dfrac{3}{5} = 2\dfrac{7}{25} +$

$1\dfrac{15}{25} = 3\dfrac{22}{25}$

[Addition of Fractions]

15. B $3\dfrac{7}{8} \div \dfrac{1}{6} = \dfrac{31}{8} \times \dfrac{6}{1} =$

$\dfrac{186}{8} = 23\dfrac{2}{8} = 23\dfrac{1}{4}$

[Division of Fractions]

16. H $\dfrac{4}{7} - \dfrac{3}{7} = \dfrac{1}{7}$

[Subtraction of Fractions]

Lesson 12 Addition of Integers (page 39)

1. C
$8 + {}^-3 = {}^+8 - 3 = 5$

2. J
${}^-4 + 9 = 5$

3. D
$9 + {}^-2 = 9 - 2 = 7$

4. H
$4 + {}^-6 = 4 - 6 = {}^-2$

5. B
${}^-9 + 13 = 4$

6. J
$10 + {}^-7 = 10 - 7 = 3$

7. E
${}^-8 + 8 = 0$

8. G
$3 + {}^-9 = 3 - 9 = {}^-6$

9. E
${}^-7 + 5 = {}^-2$

10. F
${}^-8 + 7 = {}^-1$

Lesson 13 Subtraction of Integers (page 41)

1. A
$27 - {}^-5 = 27 + {}^+5 = 32$

2. G
$7 - {}^-8 = 7 + {}^+8 = 15$

3. C $\ {}^-9 - 16 = {}^-25$

4. F
$8 - {}^-5 = 8 + {}^+5 = 13$

5. C
$28 - {}^-3 = 28 + {}^+3 = 31$

6. K
${}^-8 - 13 = {}^-21$

7. C
$3 - {}^-10 = 3 + {}^+10 = 13$

8. K
$18 - {}^-4 = 18 + {}^+4 = 22$

9. A
$3 - {}^-7 = 3 + {}^+7 = 10$

10. F
${}^-5 - 15 = {}^-20$

Lesson 14 Multiplication of Integers (page 43)

1. A
$6 \times {}^-8 = {}^-48$

2. G
${}^-4 \times {}^-15 = 60$

3. E
${}^-12 \times {}^-4 = 48$

4. F
$7 \times {}^-7 = {}^-49$

5. C
${}^-6 \times 9 = {}^-54$

6. J
$7 \times {}^-8 = {}^-56$

7. D
${}^-5 \times 8 = {}^-40$

8. K
${}^-7 \times {}^-4 = 28$

9. D
${}^-8 \times {}^-12 = 96$

10. G
$15 \times 15 = 225$

Lesson 15 Division of Integers (page 45)

1. B $\ {}^-72 \div {}^-6 =$

$$\begin{array}{r} 12 \\ 6\overline{)72} \\ \underline{-6} \\ 12 \\ \underline{-12} \\ 0 \end{array}$$

2. K $^-96 \div {}^-12 = 12\overline{)96}$

$\phantom{12\overline{)}}8$

$\phantom{12\overline{)}}\underline{-\ 96}$

$\phantom{12\overline{)96}}0$

3. C $96 \div {}^-8 = -8\overline{)96}$

$\phantom{-8\overline{)}}-12$

$\phantom{-8\overline{)}}\underline{-\ 8}$

$\phantom{-8\overline{)}}16$

$\phantom{-8\overline{)}}\underline{-\ 16}$

$\phantom{-8\overline{)96}}0$

4. H $80 \div {}^-10 = -10\overline{)80}$

$\phantom{-10\overline{)}}-8$

$\phantom{-10\overline{)}}\underline{-\ 80}$

$\phantom{-10\overline{)80}}0$

5. C $^-85 \div {}^-17 = 17\overline{)85}$

$\phantom{17\overline{)}}5$

$\phantom{17\overline{)}}\underline{-\ 85}$

$\phantom{17\overline{)85}}0$

6. K $^-92 \div 4 = 4\overline{)92}$

$\phantom{4\overline{)}}-23$

$\phantom{4\overline{)}}\underline{-\ 8}$

$\phantom{4\overline{)}}12$

$\phantom{4\overline{)}}\underline{-\ 12}$

$\phantom{4\overline{)92}}0$

[Opposite signs = negative answer]

7. B $84 \div {}^-7 = -7\overline{)84}$

$\phantom{-7\overline{)}}-12$

$\phantom{-7\overline{)}}\underline{-\ 7}$

$\phantom{-7\overline{)}}14$

$\phantom{-7\overline{)}}\underline{-\ 14}$

$\phantom{-7\overline{)84}}0$

8. F $^-72 \div 18 = 18\overline{)72}$

$\phantom{18\overline{)}}-4$

$\phantom{18\overline{)}}\underline{-\ 72}$

$\phantom{18\overline{)72}}0$

[Opposite signs = negative answer]

9. A $^-63 \div {}^-3 = 3\overline{)63}$

$\phantom{3\overline{)}}21$

$\phantom{3\overline{)}}\underline{-\ 6}$

$\phantom{3\overline{)}}03$

$\phantom{3\overline{)}}\underline{-\ 3}$

$\phantom{3\overline{)63}}0$

[Opposite signs = negative answer]

10. G $^-72 \div 24 = 24\overline{)72}$

$\phantom{24\overline{)}}-3$

$\phantom{24\overline{)}}\underline{-\ 72}$

$\phantom{24\overline{)72}}0$

[Opposite signs = negative answer]

---

1. B $30 - {}^-5 = 30 + 5 = 35$

[Subtraction of Integers]

2. J $^-80 \div {}^-5 = 5\overline{)80}$

$\phantom{5\overline{)}}16$

$\phantom{5\overline{)}}\underline{-\ 5}$

$\phantom{5\overline{)}}30$

$\phantom{5\overline{)}}\underline{-\ 30}$

$\phantom{5\overline{)80}}0$

[Division of Integers]

3. B $^-9 + 4 = {}^-5$

[Addition of Integers]

4. F $4 - {}^-9 = 4 + 9 = 13$

[Subtraction of Integers]

5. E $^-99 \div {}^-11 = 11\overline{)99}$

$\phantom{11\overline{)}}9$

$\phantom{11\overline{)}}\underline{-\ 99}$

$\phantom{11\overline{)99}}0$

[Division of Integers]

6. H $7 + {}^-9 = 7 - 9 = {}^-2$

[Addition of Integers]

7. D $^-65 \div {}^-5 = 5\overline{)65}$

$\phantom{5\overline{)}}13$

$\phantom{5\overline{)}}\underline{-\ 5}$

$\phantom{5\overline{)}}15$

$\phantom{5\overline{)}}\underline{-\ 15}$

$\phantom{5\overline{)65}}0$

[Division of Integers]

8. J $^-4 - 18 = {}^-22$

[Subtraction of Integers]

9. C $5 \times {}^-6 = {}^-30$

[Multiplication of Integers]

10. H $8 \times {}^-4 = {}^-32$

[Multiplication of Integers]

11. A $60 \div {}^-15 = -15\overline{)60}$

$\phantom{-15\overline{)}}-4$

$\phantom{-15\overline{)}}\underline{-\ 60}$

$\phantom{-15\overline{)60}}0$

[Division of Integers]

12. K $5 + {}^-4 = 5 - 4 = 1$

[Addition of Integers]

13. B $26 - {}^-3 = 26 + 3 = 29$

[Subtraction of Integers]

---

14. K $^-76 \div 4 = 4\overline{)76}$

$\phantom{4\overline{)}}-19$

$\phantom{4\overline{)}}\underline{-\ 4}$

$\phantom{4\overline{)}}36$

$\phantom{4\overline{)}}\underline{-\ 36}$

$\phantom{4\overline{)76}}0$

[Opposite signs = negative answer]

[Division of Integers]

15. D $^-6 + 8 = 2$

[Addition of Integers]

16. F $^-7 - 4 = {}^-11$

[Subtraction of Integers]

17. A $6 + {}^-10 = 6 - 10 = {}^-4$

[Addition of Integers]

18. F $84 \div {}^-21 = -21\overline{)84}$

$\phantom{-21\overline{)}}-4$

$\phantom{-21\overline{)}}\underline{-\ 84}$

$\phantom{-21\overline{)84}}0$

[Division of Integers]

19. C $^-3 + 11 = 8$

[Addition of Integers]

20. G $^-3 - 11 = {}^-14$

[Subtraction of Integers]

---

1. C

50% of $\$9.00 = 0.5 \times 9 =$

9.0

$\underline{\times\ \ \ 0.5}$

$\$4.50$

2. J 70% of $54 = 0.7 \times 54 =$

2

54

$\underline{\times\ \ 0.7}$

37.8

3. A 40% of $90 = 90$

$\underline{\times\ \ 0.4}$

36.0

4. G 100% of $76 = 1 \times 76 = 76$

5. D 80% of $\$10 = 0.8 \times 10 =$

10

$\underline{\times\ \ \ 0.8}$

$\$8.00$

---

6. J 20% of 50 =

$$\begin{array}{r} 50 \\ \times\ 0.2 \\ \hline 10.0 \end{array}$$

7. A 60% of 100 = 0.6 × 100 =

$$\begin{array}{r} 100 \\ \times\ 0.6 \\ \hline 60 \end{array}$$

8. F 100% of 83 = 83

9. E 90% of 80 =

$$\begin{array}{r} 80 \\ \times\ 0.9 \\ \hline 72.0 \end{array}$$

10. J 1% of 72 = 0.01 × 72 =

$$\begin{array}{r} 72 \\ \times\ 0.01 \\ \hline 0.72 \end{array}$$

Lesson 17 Percents—Finding the Whole or Percent (page 53)

1. B 40% of □ = 32

→ 0.4 × □ = 32

→ 32 ÷ 0.4 = 4)‾3‾2‾0‾.‾0‾ = 80.0

2. G What percent of 100 is 70?

→ □% × 100 = 70

→ 70 ÷ 100 =

100)‾7‾0‾.‾0‾ = 70%   (0.7)

3. D 24% of □ = 72

→ 0.24 × □ = 72

→ 72 ÷ 0.24 =

→ 24)‾7‾2‾0‾0‾   (300)

4. K 20% of □ = 54

→ 0.2 × □ = 54

→ 54 ÷ 0.2 = 2)‾5‾4‾0‾   (270)

---

5. C What percent of 90 is 99?

→ □% × 90 = 99

→ 99 ÷ 90 =

90)‾9‾9‾.‾0‾ = 110%   (1.1)

6. F 13% of □ = 91

→ 0.13 × □ = 91

→ 91 ÷ 0.13 =

→ 13)‾9‾1‾0‾0‾   (700)

7. C What percent of 400 is 80?

→ □% × 400 = 80

→ 80 ÷ 400 =

400)‾8‾0‾.‾0‾ = 20%   (0.2)

8. K 70% of □ = 70

→ 0.7 × □ = 70

→ 70 ÷ 0.7 = 100

TABE Review: Percents (pages 54–55)

1. B 100% of $8.50 = 1 × 8.5 = $8.50
[Percents—Finding the Part]

2. K What percent of 300 is 90?

→ □% × 300 = 90

→ 90 ÷ 300 =

300)‾9‾0‾.‾0‾ = 30%   (0.3)

[Percents—Finding the Whole or Percent]

3. A 80% of □ = 56

→ 0.8 × □ = 56

→ 56 ÷ 0.8 = 8)‾5‾6‾0‾.‾0‾   (70.0)

[Percents—Finding the Whole or Percent]

4. J

50% of 40 = 0.5 × 40 = 20.0
[Percents—Finding the Part]

---

5. A What percent of 60 is 96?

→ □% × 60 = 96

→ 96 ÷ 60 =

60)‾9‾6‾.‾0‾ = 160%   (1.6)

[Percents—Finding the Whole or Percent]

6. H 30% of 28 = 0.3 × 28 =

$$\begin{array}{r} \overset{2}{28} \\ \times\ 0.3 \\ \hline 8.4 \end{array}$$

[Percents—Finding the Part]

7. C 15% of □ = 75

→ 0.15 × □ = 75

→ 75 ÷ 0.15 =

→ 15)‾7‾5‾0‾0‾   (500)

[Percents—Finding the Whole or Percent]

8. F 90% of $1.70 = 0.9 × 1.7 =

$$\begin{array}{r} \overset{6}{1.7} \\ \times\ 0.9 \\ \hline \$1.53 \end{array}$$

[Percents—Finding the Part]

9. D 70% of □ = 91

→ 0.7 × □ = 91

→ 91 ÷ 0.7 = 7)‾9‾1‾0‾   (130)

[Percents—Finding the Whole or Percent]

10. H 50% of □ = 45

→ 0.5 × □ = 45

→ 45 ÷ 0.5 = 5)‾4‾5‾0‾   (90)

[Percents—Finding the Whole or Percent]

11. B 80% of 20 =
0.8 × 20 = 16.0
[Percents—Finding the Part]

12. F 100% of 43 = 1 × 43 = 43
[Percents—Finding the Part]

13. B What percent of 50 is 65?

$\rightarrow \square\% \times 50 = 65$

$\rightarrow 65 \div 50 = 50\overline{)65.0}^{\,1.3}$

$= 130\%$

[Percents—Finding the Whole or Percent]

14. H 1% of 3.70 = 0.01 × 3.7 = 0.037
[Percents—Finding the Part]

15. E 11% of $\square$ = 88

$\rightarrow 0.11 \times \square = 88$

$\rightarrow 88 \div 0.11 =$

$\rightarrow 11\overline{)8800}^{\,800}$

[Percents—Finding the Whole or Percent]

16. J 80% of 100 = 0.8 × 100 = 80
[Percents—Finding the Part]

17. B 10% of 60 = 0.1 × 60 = 6.0
[Percents—Finding the Part]

18. J 20% of $\square$ = 12

$\rightarrow 0.2 \times \square = 12$

$\rightarrow 12 \div 0.2 = 2\overline{)120.0}^{\,60.0}$

[Percents—Finding the Whole or Percent]

Performance Assessment (page 56)

Sample A.

D $\begin{array}{r} 42 \\ +10 \\ \hline 52 \end{array}$

1. C $\begin{array}{r} \overset{3}{64} \\ \times\ \ 9 \\ \hline 576 \end{array}$ [Multiplication of Whole Numbers—Regrouping]

2. H $\begin{array}{r} 46 \\ 6\overline{)276} \\ -24 \\ \hline 36 \\ -36 \\ \hline 0 \end{array}$ [Division of Whole Numbers—No Remainder]

3. E $\begin{array}{r} \overset{3}{491} \\ \times\ \ \ 4 \\ \hline 1964 \end{array}$ [Multiplication of Whole Numbers—Regrouping]

4. G $\begin{array}{r} 23 \\ 4\overline{)92} \\ -8 \\ \hline 12 \\ -12 \\ \hline 0 \end{array}$ [Division of Whole Numbers—No Remainder]

5. C $\begin{array}{r} \overset{5\ 13}{4.6\cancel{3}} \\ -\ 4.19 \\ \hline 0.44 \end{array}$ [Subtraction of Decimals]

6. H $\begin{array}{r} 6.2 \\ +\ 2.4 \\ \hline 8.6 \end{array}$ [Addition of Decimals]

(page 57)

7. E $\begin{array}{r} 6 \\ 15\overline{)90} \\ -90 \\ \hline 0 \end{array}$ [Division of Whole Numbers—No Remainder]

8. F $\begin{array}{r} \overset{4\ 2}{563} \\ \times\ \ \ 70 \\ \hline 39410 \end{array}$ [Multiplication of Whole Numbers—Regrouping]

9. D $\begin{array}{r} 8\ R1 \\ 4\overline{)33} \\ -32 \\ \hline 1 \end{array}$ [Division of Whole Numbers—Remainder]

10. H $\begin{array}{r} \overset{1}{\underset{}{\overset{4}{46}}} \\ \times\ \ \ 37 \\ \hline \overset{1}{322} \\ +1380 \\ \hline 1702 \end{array}$ [Multiplication of Whole Numbers—Regrouping]

11. B $^-96 \div\ ^-16 = 16\overline{)96}^{\,6}$
$\begin{array}{r} -96 \\ \hline 0 \end{array}$
[Division of Integers]

12. J $\begin{array}{r} 8.421 \\ +\ 0.363 \\ \hline 8.784 \end{array}$ [Addition of Decimals]

13. A $\dfrac{4}{5} \times \dfrac{8}{1} = \dfrac{32}{5} = 6\dfrac{2}{5}$

[Multiplication of Fractions]

14. K 20% of $5.40 =

$0.2 \times 5.4 = \begin{array}{r} 5.4 \\ \times\ 0.2 \\ \hline \$1.08 \end{array}$

[Percents—Finding the Part]

15. B 40% of $\square$ = 84

$\rightarrow 0.4 \times \square = 84$

$\rightarrow 84 \div 0.4 = 4\overline{)840}^{\,210}$
$\begin{array}{r} -8 \\ \hline 4 \\ -4 \\ \hline 00 \end{array}$

[Percents—Finding the Whole or Percent]

16. G $\dfrac{7}{8} - \dfrac{1}{8} = \dfrac{6}{8} = \dfrac{3}{4}$

[Subtraction of Fractions]

17. A 50% of 57 = 0.5 × 57 =

$\begin{array}{r} \overset{3}{57} \\ \times\ 0.5 \\ \hline 28.5 \end{array}$

[Percents—Finding the Part]

(page 58)

18. H $\dfrac{8}{13} + \dfrac{5}{13} = \dfrac{13}{13} = 1$

[Addition of Fractions]

19. D $5\dfrac{3}{4} + 8\dfrac{4}{5} =$

$5\dfrac{15}{20} + 8\dfrac{16}{20} =$

$13\dfrac{31}{20} = 14\dfrac{11}{20}$

[Addition of Fractions]

20. G $6 + {}^-3 = 6 - 3 = 3$
[Addition of Integers]

21. C $^-8 \times\ ^-6 = 48$
[Multiplication of Integers]

22. J

$$\begin{array}{r} \overset{1}{} 2.6 \\ \times 3.1 \\ \hline \overset{1}{} \\ 26 \\ + 780 \\ \hline 8.06 \end{array}$$ [Multiplication of Decimals]

23. E   What percent of 40 is 96?

→ ☐ % × 40 = 96

→ 96 ÷ 40 =

$$\begin{array}{r} 2.4 \\ 40\overline{)96.0} = 240\% \\ -80 \\ \hline 160 \\ -160 \\ \hline 0 \end{array}$$

[Percents—Finding the Whole or Percent]

24. F

$$\begin{array}{r} 1200.0 \\ 082\overline{)98400.0} \\ -82 \\ \hline 164 \\ -164 \\ \hline 0 \end{array}$$ [Division of Decimals]

25. B   ⁻6 − 14 = ⁻20

[Subtraction of Integers]